Enterprise Integration with Azure Logic Apps

Integrate legacy systems with innovative solutions

Matthew Bennett

BIRMINGHAM—MUMBAI

Enterprise Integration with Azure Logic Apps

Group Product Manager: Wilson Dsouza
Publishing Product Manager: Rahul Nair
Senior Editor: Arun Nadar
Content Development Editor: Sulagna Mohanty
Technical Editor: Shruthi Shetty
Copy Editor: Safis Editing
Project Coordinator: Shagun Saini
Proofreader: Safis Editing
Indexer: Pratik Shirodkar
Production Designer: Vijay Kamble

First published: November 2021

Production reference: 1170921

Published by Packt Publishing Ltd.
Livery Place
35 Livery Street
Birmingham
B3 2PB, UK.

ISBN 978-1-80107-472-8

www.packt.com

Foreword

The world is moving in new ways – faster, more flexible, you could say "disruptive" ways.

Progress in many fields is now made with less time refining the design and more time building, trying, evaluating, and building again better.

You wouldn't build a rocket over many years, with every detail designed to the nth degree, only to find that it doesn't work when you finally test it. You'd build a rocket in a few months, launch it, see what worked and what failed, and then build a better rocket and try again. The overall result is both better and quicker to reach.

In IT systems development, this is also becoming the case. Old server-based middleware solutions are making way for cloud-based "no-code" integrations and workflows, with quick deployment and easy improvement and adjustment to fit in with the more agile project workspace. This is where Azure Logic Apps comes in, allowing faster and more flexible development of no- or low-code solutions.

Azure Logic Apps can be used to create, develop, and deploy automated cloud-based workflows, using pre-created components with little effort and little code. These workflows can integrate your data, services, apps, CRM, and ERP in a highly scalable way, and quickly get your systems working together efficiently. But you can't just start from zero. If you're going to build and launch a rocket to see which bits work, you need to know and draw on sound engineering principles and use them in new ways.

It is the same with logic apps; you need to know and understand the tools, to quickly build the workflows and gain the benefits. You need some sort of guide.

Matthew Bennett is a senior cloud developer with experience in many business systems areas, from the Azure cloud to programming, from AX to BI. He also has a vast amount of experience in IT training at all levels, and with all types of learners. He has used this real-world and training experience combined to create another of his straightforward, easy-to-follow study guides, this time for Azure Logic Apps.

The guide takes you step by step through the aspects of creating workflows, connectors, triggers, and the actions that make up the logic app environment, as well as the knowledge needed for the supporting cloud environment.

There are plenty of hands-on tutorials, projects, step-by-step examples, scenarios, and tips to help you get to grips with the concepts.

To achieve this, the guide also covers related areas of the Azure portal, understanding the environment and resource groups, managing the cloud tenancy, development, testing and production, working with JSON, extracting data with SQL, manipulating simple and complex data, and many other tricks and tips.

Although a low-code solution, there is still some "programming-like" stuff to be familiar with, and the tutorials take you through the required parts of JSON, XML, SQL, REST, APIs, and others, while using them to work with complex data, use variables and data types, and so on.

Once these tools are understood and practiced, you will be able to quickly implement your own logic apps to integrate and automate.

Whether we are talking about a workflow as simple as sending an email or alert when a new file is uploaded, or a more complex workflow routing and processing new customer orders across separate on-premises and cloud services, all while extracting data from an old database system, with the results entered in the new systems, it all becomes possible with a little practice.

So, whether you're looking to automate your current system, interface an old system in a new system, or just learn new techniques, this guide will help you get there.

Tim Childe FLPI

Head of Teaching and Learning, Netcom Training Ltd

Contributors

About the author

Matthew Bennett is an experienced IT author, Microsoft Corporate Trainer, and former IT teacher, having been involved in the IT sector for 22 years. He currently works at Platform Housing Group, a national housing association, and creates cloud applications for a living. He has worked on integration between legacy systems and CRM products for the past 2 years but has specialized in Dynamics since 2008. Matthew studied for postgraduate diplomas in management studies and sound design, originally planning to work in film, but fell into a successful career in IT and has not looked back since. "Every day is a learning day" is his motto, and when he joined Pearson, who share the same motto, he was convinced that he was in the right profession.

About the reviewers

Bhavani Sikarwar is a seasoned integration specialist with 9 years' experience in various integration technologies, including Microsoft BizTalk Server, Azure Integration Services, and MuleSoft, He holds a Bachelor of Engineering degree in electronics and telecommunication and several industry-recognized certifications, including Azure Solution Architect, Azure DevOps Engineer, and Azure Developer Associate. He now works as an integration architect, focusing on cloud integration and helping organizations and customers build robust and reliable middleware solutions.

He has also worked on many crucial projects for banking and healthcare-based customers, including ICICI Bank and Obamacare.

I would like to thank my family and friends for their continued support and encouragement in everything that I do. You have always pushed me toward new adventures, helping me to accomplish my goals, and do what is right. I genuinely appreciate what you have done for me, and I love you.

I would also like to thank Packt Publishing for the opportunity to review this wonderful book.

Hitesh Kacholiya is a technology enthusiast and learner with over 13 years' experience in IT. He is currently working as an enterprise cloud solutions architect at a leading energy technology company. He has been working in Microsoft Technologies for almost his entire career and has experienced the technology shifts that have occurred firsthand. As part of migrations, modernizations, and transformations, he has worked on new technologies such as the cloud, IAC, Terraform, Bot Framework, Logic Apps, Azure Functions, and ServiceNow, to name but a few. He has a bachelor's degree in engineering and a lot of certifications from Microsoft, Scaled Agile, and Amazon, including MAPA Champs for Azure and Office 365. Outside of work, he enjoys cricket and music.

I've always put my family first and that's just the way it is! Thank you for putting up with me, my long work and study hours, and always being there for me.

Special thanks to my better half, Varsha, my mom, Deepa, and my sister, Ankisha, for enabling me to be where I am in my life right now.

To my children, Mishka and Miransh: You are the center of my universe.

To my dad: I hope I have made you proud because that's all I ever wanted to do! I'll always miss you.

Table of Contents

3

Referencing Data within Actions

4

Reading Complex Data

5

Manipulating Data

Section 2: Logic App Design

6

Working with the Common Data Service

7

Working with Azure Functions

8

Scoping with Try/Catch Error Handling

Section 3: Logic App Maintenance and Management

Preface

Microsoft logic apps are new and powerful tools for bulk data processing and system integration that help you harness data manipulation through visual flowcharts. This book will enable you to integrate old and new systems seamlessly for back-office operations and create management reports to analyze the health of your logic.

Who this book is for

If you are an aspiring infrastructure technician who already uses Azure in place of on-premises solutions and is now looking to link systems together, then this book is for you. This book is also for developers interested in system integration where legacy systems may not have a direct data link and the cloud is the intermediary step. Power users with existing IT skills and experience with Power BI and Power Automate will also find this book useful.

What this book covers

Chapter 1, *Getting Started with Azure Logic Apps*, introduces Azure to new readers but serves as a reference tool for Azure users. It describes how to obtain an MSDN account and manage the subscription and provides a walk-through of the Azure portal as it relates to logic apps. This chapter contains step-by-step guides to demonstrate how to set up a new account.

Chapter 2, *Environments and Resource Groups*, introduces the concept of resource groups as a way of separating Azure objects based on their use, for example, the creation of resource group environments for sandboxing, development, testing, user-acceptance testing, and production pipelines so that new logic can be tested as part of a managed solution.

Chapter 3, *Referencing Data within Actions*, explains how to initialize, and set a variable, and how to parameterize a JSON message to obtain field data. You will then learn the difference between the logical field name and the physical field name.

Chapter 4, Reading Complex Data, shows you how to access specific fields from an array, an object, and from a table using the parsing parameterization process.

Chapter 5, Manipulating Data, covers how to perform calculations, concatenate text, split a string, count the length of a string, and index the position of a word or character within a string.

Chapter 6, Working with the Common Data Service, looks at how to retrieve and update records in third-party systems and databases using the web-based Common Data Service series of actions.

Chapter 7, Working with Azure Functions, addresses the fact that although logic apps allow you to perform most common actions, some more complex manipulation may require a C# app. This chapter looks at how you can use your functions within a logic app.

Chapter 8, Scoping with Try/Catch Error Handling, looks at how, as the complexity of the logic grows, it would be sensible to divide the flowchart into different sections. The scope feature allows you to be able to do this, reducing clutter on the flowchart. Output from a scope can also be obtained for debugging purposes. The scope feature has the further use of being able to focus the developer's attention on problematic code. Output and error messages from this section can be obtained and debugged, with further remedial action taken when errors do occur.

Chapter 9, Sharing Data with Other Logic Apps and APIs, looks at how we can link logic apps together and share data between them. As logic apps grow ever more complex, we can build them with reusable code parts. Common, repeatable logic can be used time and again by a series of other "parent" logic apps.

Chapter 10, Monitoring Logic Apps for Management Reporting, walks you through the Logic Apps creation wizard and explains how Log Analytics is used to be able to produce real-time reporting on resource group objects, providing a holistic overview of logic health within the monitored environment. By doing this, the developer can easily track errors in the logic, how often the problem is occurring, and where the fault is located.

Chapter 11, Fine-Tuning Logic App Runs with Run After, explores how the process of creating and fine-tuning a logic app depends on knowing what data you are expecting to see, the format you want that data to end up using, and adding conditions to check that operationally, procedurally, or programmatically related data can also be obtained, manipulated, and used as efficiently as possible. Sometimes, you only want a certain section of a logic app to work if the previous action was successful, or failed, or was skipped. By creating different logic branches, you can do different things based on whether the action was successful or not.

Chapter 12, Solving Connection Issues and Bad Gateways by Rerunning Logic Apps, looks at how, when trying to communicate with other cloud or on-premises domains, you have to authenticate and pass data through a firewall. Logic apps have a timeout window of up to 2 minutes and presume that if no response is received before this time, the data is lost, and the connection is uncontactable. This chapter looks at common connection issues, how to understand them, and how to resolve them. As development is an iterative process, you may need to run your logic apps several times until you are happy with the result. This chapter looks at how you can rerun logic app runs without having to resend the original data from your external system time and again.

To get the most out of this book

You need to have an understanding of SQL databases and query design, along with some previous experience in basic programming and business process designing.

Software/Hardware covered in the book	OS Requirements
Other than access to a browser, there are no software requirements (although at times, Visual Studio can be used alongside Azure).	No specific OS requirements.
JSON Schema tool.	
JSON Formatter.	

Download the color images

We also provide a PDF file that has color images of the screenshots/diagrams used in this book. You can download it here: `http://www.packtpub.com/sites/default/files/downloads/9781801074728_ColorImages.pdf`.

Conventions used

There are a number of text conventions used throughout this book.

`Code in text`: Indicates code words in text, database table names, folder names, filenames, file extensions, pathnames, dummy URLs, user input, and Twitter handles. Here is an example: "This is JSON code for the `List_records` action."

A block of code is set as follows:

```
"List_records": {
                "runAfter": {},
                "type": "ApiConnection",
                "inputs": {
                    "host": {
                        "connection": {
                            "name": "@
parameters('$connections')['commondataservice']
['connectionId']"
                        }
                    },
                    "method": "get",
                    "path": "/v2/datasets/@
{encodeURIComponent(encodeURIComponent('org539840ba.crm11'))}/
tables/@{encodeURIComponent(encodeURIComponent('Persons'))}/
items",
                    "queries": {
                        "$filter": "d365_contactlocation eq
'SWINDON'"
                    }
                }
            }
```

Any command-line input or output is written as follows:

```
$ sudo tunctl -u $(whoami) -t tap0
```

Bold: Indicates a new term, an important word, or words that you see onscreen. For example, words in menus or dialog boxes appear in the text like this. Here is an example: "In the logic app, near the top of the logic app, I create a **Compose** action to store this GUID."

> **Tips or important notes**
> Appear like this.

Get in touch

Feedback from our readers is always welcome.

General feedback: If you have questions about any aspect of this book, mention the book title in the subject of your message and email us at customercare@packtpub.com.

Errata: Although we have taken every care to ensure the accuracy of our content, mistakes do happen. If you have found a mistake in this book, we would be grateful if you would report this to us. Please visit www.packtpub.com/support/errata, selecting your book, clicking on the Errata Submission Form link, and entering the details.

Piracy: If you come across any illegal copies of our works in any form on the Internet, we would be grateful if you would provide us with the location address or website name. Please contact us at copyright@packt.com with a link to the material.

If you are interested in becoming an author: If there is a topic that you have expertise in and you are interested in either writing or contributing to a book, please visit authors.packtpub.com.

Share Your Thoughts

Once you've read *Enterprise Integration with Azure Logic Apps*, we'd love to hear your thoughts! Scan the QR code below to go straight to the Amazon review page for this book and share your feedback.

https://packt.link/r/1-801-07472-0

Your review is important to us and the tech community and will help us make sure we're delivering excellent quality content.

Section 1: Logic App Fundamentals

Create sophisticated, reliable logic apps, learning to use actions and triggers. Quickly build complex and powerful logic, integrating data on demand and improving the user experience.

This part of the book comprises the following chapters:

- *Chapter 1, Getting Started with Azure Logic Apps*
- *Chapter 2, Environments and Resource Groups*
- *Chapter 3, Referencing Data within Actions*
- *Chapter 4, Reading Complex Data*
- *Chapter 5, Manipulating Data*

1
Getting Started with Azure Logic Apps

This chapter introduces us to a new way of working – the *no-code revolution*. Microsoft Azure makes this possible by taking the concept of a flowchart and applying it to the access, formatting, calculating, and use of data within systems. As a result, for the end user, **Flow**, now called **Power Automate,** was born, allowing interaction, alerting, and collaboration. For developers, logic apps was created, allowing large amounts of records in bulk form to be updated immediately upon a change, or saved in the frontend system. Immediate alterations and process logic are now possible without the need to write custom apps. These may be complex to write but can address problems within a matter of minutes, not days.

In this chapter, we're going to cover the following main topics:

- Introducing the new world
- We know the why, now for the how
- At your service
- It all leads to logic
- Introducing Azure

- Getting started with Azure Logic Apps
- Obtaining an MSDN account
- The Azure portal

Introducing the new world

IT is changing. IT is forever evolving, and in line with that, the business market adapts, evolves in turn, and enhances itself. IT used to be complex, time-consuming, and expensive. Programming had a reputation for seeming *alien* and *techy*, distancing regular people from the task – making the task ever harder to accomplish. Welcome to your first step into a new world.

As a former Microsoft Trainer, I have been watching the evolution not only of Microsoft's software as it adapts to needs but also how businesses adapt to the changing landscape. In 2016, Microsoft published its new strategy: *Digital transformation: Seven steps to success*. This highlights several changes afoot in the current climate, or as their strapline puts it, *How businesses can stay relevant and competitive in today's new digital era*. More information can be found here: `https://aka.my/3AE`.

The document explains how technology has become pervasive in modern society. How it has gone beyond the computer lab, the office, and the factory floor and into homes, fridges, and wearable devices. The **Internet of Things** (**IoT**) requires an ever-growing amount of data that is ever more complex. Moreover, we are not only interested in managing this data but are also seeking to make sense of it. Through advanced analytics, artificial intelligence, and machine learning, we can track patterns, make predictions, and determine how we can make the best decisions, or even let these technologies make them for us.

Microsoft focused on seven key areas of change:

- **Leadership matters**: Technology, and the ability to be clever enough to perform a task, does not make you a leader. By removing the technical barrier, leadership remains solely focused on vision and strategy.
- **Cultural change is driven by effective change management**: Becoming a *digital* enterprise will change how the organization makes decisions.
- **Connect your customers, products, assets, and people**: Through this connection, customers will be aware of what is being planned and can shape strategy through dialog and demand. People will be able to interact with your system seamlessly. Here, "people" refers to company staff and stakeholders, whereas customers are buyers who are not interested in the mechanics of the system you have built to sell to them.

- **Adopt a data culture**: As the amount of information required grows, the Microsoft cloud platform offers a hardware-invisible, *pay-as-you-go* solution to your data needs at all levels. The focus is less on how much upfront cost you will need to get started, or what you need to build your IT hardware infrastructure, and instead on a *turnkey* model that is provided for the business. Everything you need to get started is at your fingertips from day 1.

- **Experiment and fail fast**: By adopting short planning and implementation cycles – or even better, an Agile approach – your team can develop, test, go back a step, try again, and refine until they reach a much faster and less expensive solution. The concept of the *fail fast* and *learn fast* era means that accelerated development produces accelerated learning and maturity of the product in a much, much smaller timescale.

> **Note:**
>
> On the topic of point 5, I have experienced first-hand how, when embraced correctly, the *Experiment and fail fast* methodology can be a force for significant change within the company in many ways. I work for a large organization in the UK with a small development team that traditionally worked on highly technical programming projects. They were seen by the wider business as *experts*, and sometimes only communicated when there was an absolute need for their input. Most of the business was operational in nature, so the office was awash with administrative staff, managers, and analysts. Project work was an essential part of the change, but that change had to be embraced by the wider business. To assist with this, and as a conduit, business analysts and change officers would inspect developments and then sell these to the wider business for adoption. Project rollout was phased, per department, and over time.
>
> While all of this was happening, the developers were adopting an **Agile** approach. They quickly learned how to use Azure as the new key area for IT project development and would experiment with the use of logic apps and Power Automate (Flow) to create logic tasks, integrating systems and building the requirements that would then be tested and demonstrated by the *business change* team. The need to engage developers and change agents, plus the need to think about the solution in a more technical way, was a culture shift for the business as it planned to incorporate Agile working alongside **PRINCE2** or **Six-Sigma** project management.

- **Think ecosystem and become an enterprise software company**: The structure of the company will need to alter to embrace the changes demanded of it by wider engagements with its supply chain, providers, partners, IT systems, creditors, communication channels, and so on. Change is needed as the company goes from thinking about making a product or offering a service for one specific partner, business, or group of people, to instead adopting a holistic approach. The business is now encouraged to think *end to end* in relation to its supply chain, manufacturing, and distribution.

- **Who is my Uber?**: Through 2015-2019, I followed the legal battles between London taxi companies and their unions and Uber, the emerging company whose strategy undercut the incumbent and dominant provider. I found this to be an interesting test case – Uber had no fleet of its own, no assets, no big offices. Everything was virtualized and socially focused, and, as such, cost margins were lower and the customer, in turn, benefitted from this.

- Following on from the example of a virtual world, companies such as Amazon, eBay, Netflix, and Uber share one thing in common: they don't manufacture a product but instead offer a marketplace. If I wanted to sell an item a few decades ago, I might have held a stall at a flea market or traded it in at a pawn shop. Now, services are offered for consumers to consume without the need for handling goods, negotiation, waiting for production, and so on. This was extremely apparent last year when the UK entered the COVID-19 lockdown; everyone bought takeaways, shopped for groceries, and bought items online, *and got them delivered the next day*. We went from an *owning* society to a *renting, disposable* society, and this social and cultural shift is very important if you are a person who can operate holistically and offer an end-to-end service.

Hopefully, the paragraphs so far will have provided interesting content for you, but you are reading this book to understand not why we are where we are today, but how you can benefit from the situation, and how you can use modern change development tools and build solutions quickly and efficiently.

Forgive me, dear reader, but I don't know your skill set, your career path, or whether you have also thought about some of these seismic changes to our industry. The change is potentially so great that the expression *The King is dead, long live the King!* is rather apt. We have no choice but to change because change is inevitable.

We know the why, now for the how

Microsoft Azure was launched several years ago. As a trainer, I saw a shift in focus from infrastructure training (for example, **Microsoft Certified Systems Administrator (MCSA) 2003 Server**) to **Microsoft Certified Solutions Associate**. The system became increasingly irrelevant. Concepts such as DNS, DHCP, and subnetting/supernetting, which were highly technical, became less important. They were still in use but became merely second-nature configuration settings. For the IT development community, the focus shifted to creating **no-code application solutions**, of which system hardware and infrastructure were key parts.

The next change was the hybrid approach. This involved the coexistence of cloud (off-premises) and on-premises IT systems, with some tasks done online while others were performed with some cloud-based platforms while the internal on-premises domain remained protected. Here, the focus was on concepts such as the **demilitarized zone, web servers, and honeypots/honeynets**.

The next change was based on trust in the technology, and legal adoption, as trust was given to Microsoft Azure sites located in different countries across the globe. Concepts such as **federation**, **Single Sign-On (SSO)**, and **identity management** became the focus as IT teams merged on-premises systems with the cloud. The cloud became a *gated* area where a company could own a **tenant** (a dedicated instance of **Active Directory (AD)**) that was secure.

In the period 2015-2019, two products from Microsoft were significantly changed and became cloud based. These were Microsoft's most important and highly used enterprise applications: Office and Dynamics. Office became Office 365, Dynamics became Dynamics 365, and both used the Office 365 tenant cloud, which co-exists as part of the Azure cloud.

At your service

From these key concepts, cloud *as-a-service* offerings were launched:

- **Software as a Service (SaaS)**: This is a way of delivering your custom application as a serviceable and consumable product through the internet. Gone are the days of buying a CD-ROM containing a program that then needed to be installed locally. You can now simply navigate to a website where the application is hosted to run it. Websites (commonly termed by Microsoft as *web applications*) are an example of this.

To assist the developer further, **Visual Studio**, the main editor application suite available from Microsoft, was also made available as a cloud solution (now called Visual Studio Code).

- **Platform as a Service (PaaS)**: Some code and applications cannot run on a web server. They may still require a machine with a specific operating system to be able to function. For example, I use a variety of code packages from GitHub that are based on the Python programming language. This is a small but powerful language, but it is not web-based. Here, I would create a **Virtual Machine (VM)** and, on this, build my Python app. I can take a snapshot of the VM, clone, and then rebuild the container by, for example, using **Docker**. When the installation process is complex and multi-layered, using this simplifies the process. Docker is an excellent product that you will want to install on VMs. You will also want to use a layered software approach to share the same operating system but customize copies of the same build to be used in different ways (for example, two Linux builds with different middleware and different architecture on a virtual network).

  To get started with Docker and build your first pre-installed VM, visit the following link: `https://www.docker.com/get-started`.

- **Infrastructure as a Service (IaaS)**: Now, the entire IT hardware infrastructure can be created in the Azure cloud. Servers, firewalls, and data storage can all be *spun up* as required and on demand. You pay per use and by the amount of processing power or storage capacity you need. If managed correctly, costs can be considerably reduced as an initial outlay (the purchase of expensive hardware) is no longer required.

- **Anything as a Service (XaaS)**: As cloud offerings expand, they also incorporate interlinking and communication with various established third-party enterprise products. A mixture of services could be offered by a provider, and by doing so, allow the user the ability to create a complex solution, linking different parts of the business together, while in the process moving on-premises data and software to the cloud.

  Azure, **Google Cloud Platform**, and **Amazon Web Services** are some of the providers offering XaaS solutions.

It all leads to logic

"Logic, my dear Zoe, merely enables one to be wrong with authority."

-(Doctor Who, The Wheel in Space, 1968)

"Everything yields to logic. Our basic assumption."

-(Doctor Who, The Tomb of the Cybermen, 1967)

And so, we come to the most important tool to connect all these systems together – logic apps.

The **Microsoft Azure Logic App** is an example of *no-code* development. The idea is that a non-technical person who has not learned a programming language can still produce logic in much the same way that a business analyst may structure a sequence of events in a Visio flowchart.

> **Note**
>
> Sadly, I once lost a government teaching contract due to the change toward no-code development. I delivered a Visio training course and mentioned that the aim for Microsoft was to allow non-programmers to create program code. The initial idea was that a Visio diagram of an application would contain logic, and that could be turned into a skeleton of modules and functions within Visual Studio.
>
> Not so far out. The eventual product was Logic Apps.

Introducing Azure

Azure is the brand name for Microsoft's cloud subscription offering. It covers every possible aspect of IT. With it, you can create your own virtual networks and databases, run CRM systems, and code without the need to install coding software on your PC. You can also run your own project management teams and their project boards and run Microsoft Office from anywhere.

The possibilities are virtually endless.

The following screenshot is a section from the welcome screen of Microsoft Azure, showing the various areas that make up your Azure environment:

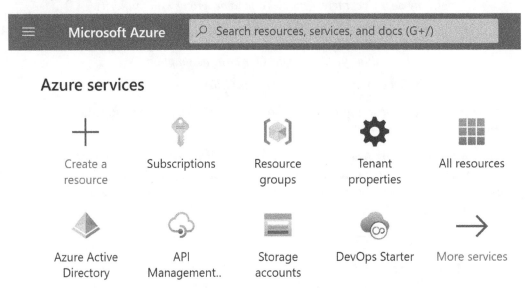

Figure 1.1 – Azure home page header containing common areas

Azure is the platform used to maintain your account and manage data and virtual objects (such as *VMs*), as well as *logic* currently housed within your account. You also have access to an editing tool that allows you to create logic to refine data, format data, and migrate or integrate data between systems. Azure operates under a subscription model, and you pay for what you use.

This logic editing tool is **Logic Apps**, a tool we will be focusing on in this book.

Key Azure terms

The following is a list of key Azure terms that you should know:

- **Tenant**: This is a private cloud environment shared by users. This is typically linked to one or more domain names. When you set up your Microsoft (Office 365) subscription, you create a tenant.

- **Subscription**: You can have one or several subscriptions linked to your Azure tenant, or one subscription can be used to pay for multiple tenants. The subscription is the financial mechanism (account) used to pay for the Azure resources consumed within the tenant. This may be on an enterprise model basis, costed plan, or *pay-as-you-go* model, depending on the extent you want to engage with Azure.

- **Resource group**: A logical grouping of objects and resources (for example, by department or by environment). You can have copies of the same resource in several different resource groups.

- **Resource objects**: These must be stored within a resource group and could be a variety of different items such as functions, logic apps, web apps, Virtual Machines, **Binary Large Object** (**BLOB**) storage, or a variety of other resources.

Getting started with Azure

As a first-time user, the following will be needed before you can get started:

1. An email account (this does not have to be a Microsoft account). I will presume you have one already.

2. A Microsoft 365 Business Basic account. This is what was originally referred to as an Office 365 account. It gives you access to the Microsoft Office suite, but also adds your user account into an authentication service called Azure AD, which is used to define what you can access and your level of access. *Visual Studio Code*, *Dynamic 365*, and *DevOps* also form part of the suite of applications available to you, as well as *Visio* and *Project*. We will look at how to set this up in the next section.

3. An Azure subscription. We will also set this up in the next section.

Setting up a Microsoft 365 Business Basic account

In this section, you will learn how to set up a Microsoft 365 Business Basic account.

Please navigate to the following link to get the most up-to-date instructions, as the sign-up process is subject to regular changes:

```
https://docs.microsoft.com/en-us/microsoft-365/admin/setup/
setup-business-basic?view=o365-worldwide
```

The sign-up instructions are listed underneath an explanatory video. Please use these to set up the account.

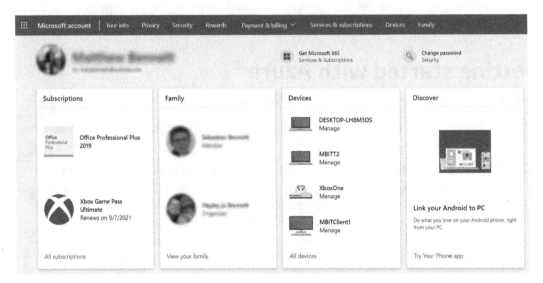

Figure 1.2 – A section of the welcome page of your Microsoft account

Your Microsoft Azure account is a collection of all the cloud objects you will create. Some of these will be used by your account for Power Automate (`https://flow.microsoft.com/`). The following website will also be used by power users, and users wishing to get started straight away, to create apps and objects that support users with your cloud infrastructure: `https://make.powerapps.com/`. The actual objects, however, are stored in the Azure account.

Getting started with Azure

Now that you have a Microsoft account and access to end user resources, we need to create a cloud environment to create your projects and logic. For this, navigate to https://portal.azure.com/ and click the **Start for free** button to begin the enrollment process.

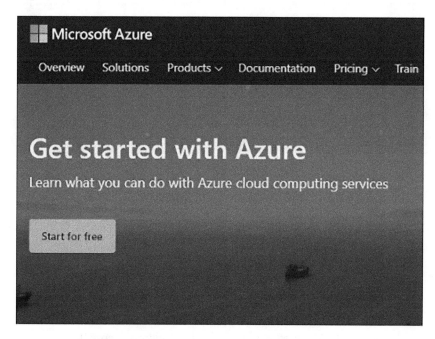

Figure 1.3 – The Azure sign-up portal

From the Azure welcome page, please take a moment to look at what is possible with the variety of Azure demo videos available here: https://azure.microsoft.com/en-gb/get-started/video/.

Setting up Azure

You will first be required to sign in, using the Microsoft account you created in the previous section. If you have a third-party email account linked to a GitHub account, you could use that, so long as it is not already tied to a Microsoft account.

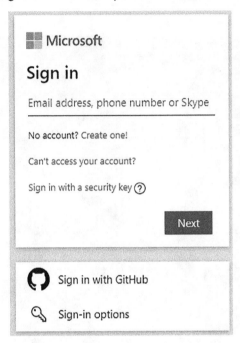

Figure 1.4 – Microsoft sign-in screen (email address removed)

Next, you will be asked to create your free Azure account. You will notice that credit is applied for your first 30 days.

> **Important note**
> If the services you create do not incur any charges, the account will be deleted after 6 months of inactivity.

The next step will require you to verify your identity using your phone.

This is then followed by financial authorization. Your card details are checked; however, you will not be charged unless you upgrade to a paid account.

Finally, read all the terms and conditions, and if you are happy, click on **Agree**.

The account will be generated, and you will then be presented with a home screen.

Before we can get started, you will need to attach a subscription to the account. Initially, you might wish to start with a *pay-as-you-go* subscription, although the credit provided on sign-up will also apply first. For myself, I already have a Microsoft MSDN Developer account, so have attached this as my Azure subscription, as shown in the following figure:

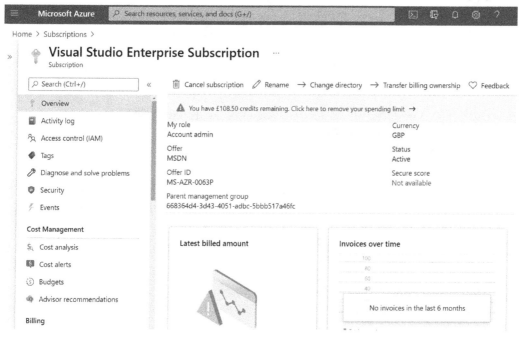

Figure 1.5 – The Subscriptions page showing my MSDN account

The **Subscriptions** page explains spending as it relates to the Azure subscription, which focuses on background objects and tasks. Any Flows or Power Automate apps (logic apps for frontend IT users) may not feature in this calculation.

Obtaining an MSDN account

This process is regularly changed by Microsoft, so a URL has not been provided. The standard MSDN URL now redirects to Microsoft Learn.

Please note that the following pricing* is indicative and subject to change:

- A **Visual Studio Community** subscription is free for non-enterprise users and for non-commercial projects. This is for people entering the industry, or students starting out in application development.

- The **MSDN Visual Studio Professional** subscription is $539/year for a cloud subscription or $1,199 for the first year of a perpetual license, with renewals at $799 per year. However, with this, you get licenses for Windows and Windows Server to be used for testing, alongside $50/month of Azure credit.

- An **MSDN Visual Studio Enterprise** subscription costs $5,999 for the first year and $2,569 for annual renewals. Volume Licensing customers get a discount at $2,999/year. For this, you get $150/month in Azure credits, a Microsoft Office Professional Plus license with full usage rights, an Office 365 Developer license, as well as Exchange, SharePoint, and Power BI Pro licenses.

- The **MSDN Visual Studio Test Professional** subscription is not intended for developers, instead, it is marketed to testers. This is only available as a perpetual license product at $2,169 for the first year, then $899 for subsequent years. This account features $50 of Azure credit each month.

- Finally, the **MSDN Platforms** subscription is available for Volume Licensing customers only. This is for IT operational staff and Java developers who will not require access to the full Visual Studio product. The subscription is $2,000 but may vary based on the reseller. It does, however, include $100 of Azure credits to spend each month.

*Sourced from TechRepublic.com, available at `https://www.techrepublic.com/article/a-quick-guide-to-choosing-the-right-msdn-subscription/`.

The Azure portal

The most obvious place to start would be the **All resources** page. This shows all hidden and visible resources on the account.

The Azure portal is your one-stop shop for everything to do with your cloud subscription. Here, you can do the following:

- Create new resources (there are several hundred different kinds available in the Microsoft catalog at present).

- Create resource groups for grouping objects.

- Manage your virtual infrastructure.

- Monitor the health of your resources.

- Check pricing levels.

- Update object performance by *scaling up*. This means that your resource will perform quicker, but for an increased cost, as more resources are provided for it to use.

- Add object reliability and *high availability* by *scaling out*. This means that your resource is always available.

Refer to the following figure:

Figure 1.6 – All resources showing connections and other visible resources

You will find yourself becoming a regular user of the Azure portal if you intend to build logic apps!

Resource groups

A resource group is a collection of objects. It typically contains objects used by just one department, one location, or a stage of development.

Typical resource group names could therefore be the following:

- **Geographical**: Such as North, South, East

- **Departmental**: Such as Research, Production, Marketing

- **Development Stages**: Such as Sandbox, Development, Testing, Production

This book is going to focus on the **staged model** – a model that is commonly used by development teams. It also aligns with the Agile model.

Here, we can see a list of **resource groups** I have created. Some are specific to a project, and others relate to an *environment stage* for an enterprise-level project:

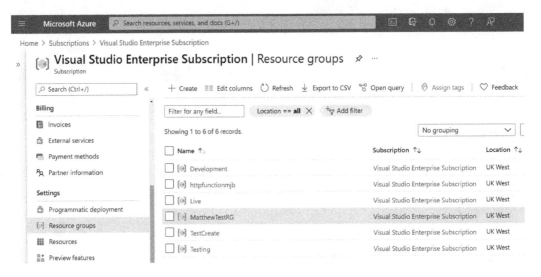

Figure 1.7 – Resource groups in my subscription

Looking at one of these groups, we can see an object (in this case, a **storage account**) that is housed within this resource group:

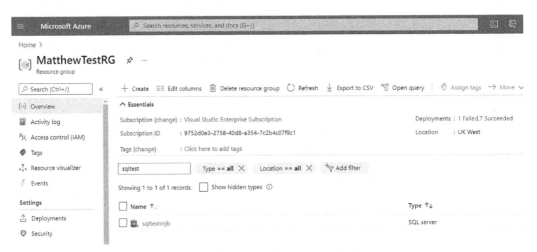

Figure 1.8 – My storage object is my first resource in the resource group

> **Tip**
> Resource groups are a logical means to separate objects based on their stage, their purpose, or any other grouping. However, it is common to create a *General* or *Core* resource group where common objects can be reused across other resource groups. For example, an Azure function could be reused by development, testing, and production resource groups.

The object home page

Each object has an overview page that illustrates the status of the object. From here, you can determine whether it is running, can start/stop the object, and can scale it up (add more processing power/storage) or scale it out (copy it to other servers to provide fault tolerance and reliability). The following figure depicts my storage overview page:

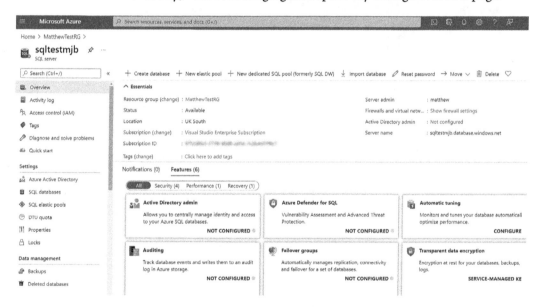

Figure 1.9 – My storage overview page

You will notice that each Azure page is highly visual and richly detailed, containing tiles for further information. Information is categorized in sections and the object is highly configurable.

Blades and slices

You will notice that each Azure page starts on the left with a panel allowing you to select the section you are interested in. This is referred to as the **blade**.

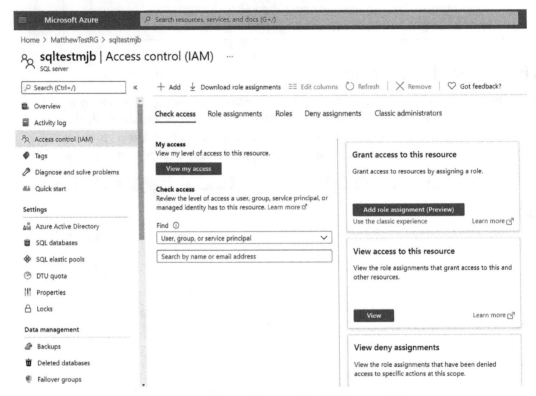

Figure 1.10 – sqltestmjb showing blades, slices, and tiles

In the preceding screenshot, you can see the storage blade showing a series of slices and tiles relating to access control for this storage object.

A blade is a starting point to determine how to customize an object.

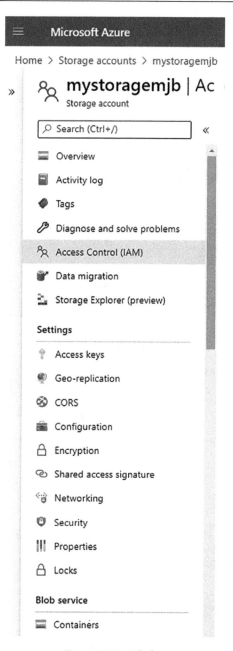

Figure 1.11 – Blade

A slice is a section detailing the options you have to customize your blade action.

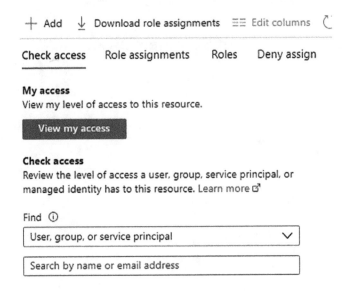

Figure 1.12 – Slice

A tile is a specific element you wish to customize.

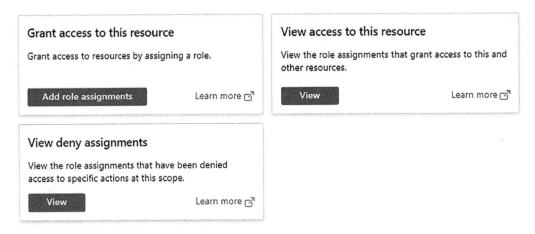

Figure 1.13 – Tiles

Each object follows this principle, and, as we turn our focus on later chapters to logic apps, you will also learn about the configurable sections of objects.

Summary

In this chapter, I shared with you some of my experiences working within IT and in noticing the fundamental shift from traditional infrastructure, on-premises programming done by experts, to a service model more widely accessible across a cloud network. The focus is less on making exclusive code and more on offering holistic end-to-end services. The marketplace is less about the individual, the supply chain, or specific customers, and is now open to anyone and everyone, at a global level.

We then looked at how to get started by creating a Microsoft 365 account, an MSDN subscription (where this is needed), and an Azure subscription. We looked at the current costs, advantages, and disadvantages, at the time of writing this book. We then took a deep dive into the Azure user interface to understand resources, resource groups, subscriptions, and the notion of a tenant.

Finally, I showed one object (deliberately not a logic app, as these will be covered in later chapters in some detail) and encouraged you to understand the common structure of the Azure resource object panes. I mentioned that an object is split into separate pages and that these pages are accessible via the leftmost blade. Each blade expands from left to right, and each section contains the stages to develop and customize the object further.

Now that you have an Azure account and are familiarizing yourself with the environment, in the next chapter, we will be looking at the resource group in further detail and considering how you can plan an enterprise environment within your tenant.

2
Environments and Resource Groups

This chapter is designed to introduce the concept of **resource groups** as a way of separating Azure objects based on their use, for example, the creation of resource group environments for sandbox, development, testing, user acceptance testing, and production pipelines so that new logic can be tested as part of a managed solution. This chapter will explain how projects or work areas can be separated within Azure.

In this chapter, you will learn how to do the following:

- Manage the cloud tenant effectively.
- Create a series of resource groups to separate different versions of the same object across the environment, zoning your objects to allow development, testing, and production to exist separately.
- Create clones of resources manually to allow for a development life cycle from sandbox through to production.

The chapter will cover the following areas:

- Separating the cloud
- Creating resource groups
- Moving resources

Technical requirements

The following are the technical requirements for the chapter:

- Other than access to a browser, there are no software requirements (although at times, Visual Studio can be used alongside Azure).

- An understanding of SQL databases and query design.

- Some previous experience of basic programming (although we are using a no-code solution).

- Some experience in business process design.

Separating the cloud

Over time, your team will be using a series of subscriptions to pay for Azure resources but will be working within one tenant. A **tenancy** is the overall Azure account in which you can have multiple developers sharing the Azure space.

To understand an overview of the Azure space, we will start from the *home* page. Log in to your Azure account at `https://portal.azure.com/#home`.

To log in, please use the Microsoft account linked to your MSDN subscription. This is explained in *Chapter 1, Getting Started with Azure Logic Apps*.

> TIP
> At the time of writing, Microsoft offers credit to new accounts. I currently get over £100/month as part of my MSDN subscription to get started with Azure.

The following screenshot shows the home page layout for Microsoft Azure:

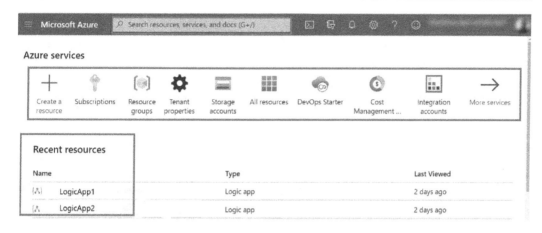

Figure 2.1 – The current home page layout

In the preceding screenshot, three areas of interest are highlighted:

- The *global search* is present on the blue bar at the top of the screen. This will show any existing resources and suggestions of new resources that share the same name as your search keyword or phrase.

- The **Azure services** section lists common tasks and key areas of the account. The most used is the **Resource groups** button.

- The most recently accessed resources are displayed in the **Recent resources** list. Clicking on the resource will take you to the overview page for that resource.

Let's now discuss what constitutes a resource. A **resource** is a general term for an object in Azure. Typical resources include the following:

- Storage account
- Integration service
- Virtual machine
- Database
- Logic app
- Kubernetes service

By pressing **Create a resource** in the **Azure services** section, you will be presented with the **Azure Marketplace** catalog, which contains several hundred objects to choose from, as shown in the following screenshot:

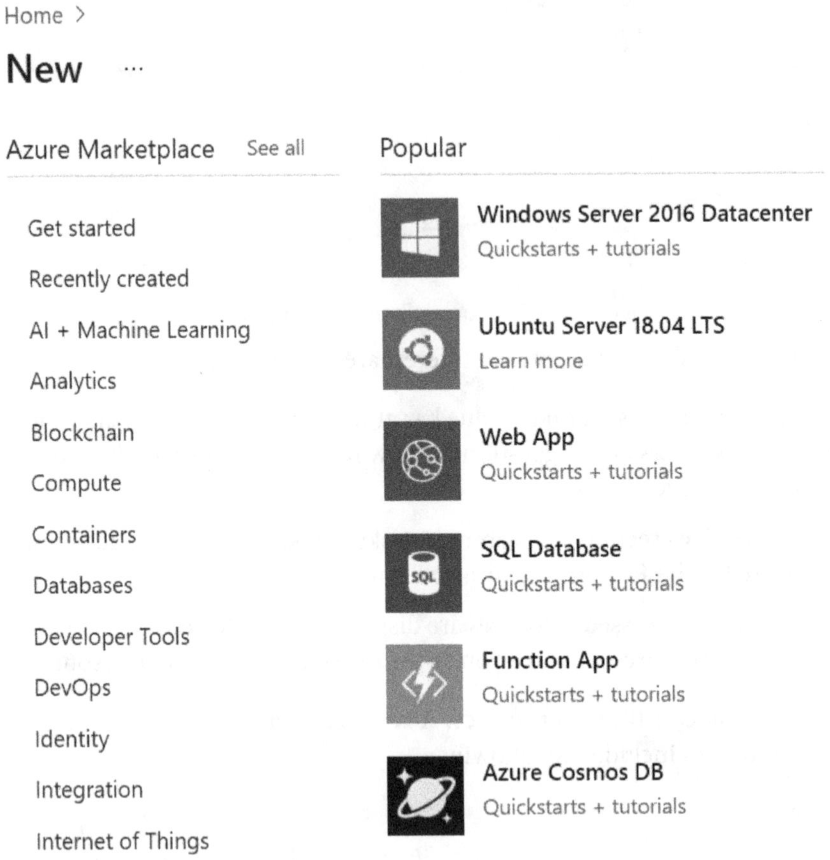

Figure 2.2 – The Azure Marketplace catalog has a wide variety of tools and resources

Therefore, over time, the Azure cloud will be populated with a variety of resources covering multiple projects. To manage these efficiently, you must create a resource group for each project or project stage.

Let's look at what we mean by a resource group and how we can use this to logically partition our Azure objects into projects, phases, departments, geographical regions, or any other structure you see fit.

Creating resource groups

In this section, we are going to look at how we can use a resource group to structure our Azure clouds. We will consider what a resource group is and how to plan to use them in the real world and will then look at a practical example of how to create a resource group.

What is a resource group?

A **resource group** is a logical section of Azure in which you can add resources. Typically, a resource group would be created to hold all objects relating to the same project. For example, a logic app may need a database to store data while it performs its run. Similarly, files may need to be created because of a logic app's run.

Before an object can be created, you are asked which resource group to place the new object into, as a mandatory requirement of the object creation form. If you are creating an Azure function and decide to use the basic **Publish** wizard, a resource group with the project objects is created with the same name as the project. This will be covered in the exercise in *Chapter 7, Working with Azure Functions*.

> TIP
>
> Azure functions are one of several objects that must be uniquely named within the Azure tenant. This is at variance with what we will now see with other object types, which deliberately share the same name.

Finally, you might want to consider a **core** resource group. You may have resources such as logic apps that will call a **workhorse** function that is used many times by different resources. Here, you would only need to make the function once – it will be available to be scoped to anywhere within your Azure space. This, however, is at odds with the logical partitioning we discussed previously, but the decision is up to you. Core resource groups can make your Azure space more efficient and easier to maintain.

Planning your resource groups

It is best to design environment areas for each project and in the event of enterprise-level projects where you will have a staged approach to your development tasks, it is customary to have mirror images of your **Customer Relationship Management** (**CRM**) environment for each team to work on separately, where changes can be tested and then brought into the live environment by copying resources from one resource group to another.

As a bare minimum, a typical environment architecture for the project would be as follows:

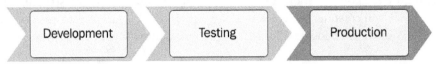

Figure 2.3 – The basic enterprise staged model in line with the Agile process

In this model, we will create a series of objects such as logic apps first in the development resource group, labeled and tagged to explain the purpose of the task it will perform. The naming convention is as follows:

- Determine the overall **Create, Read, Update, and Delete (CRUD)** action of the logic app (such as are we *creating* a record, *updating* a record, or *deleting* a record?).

- Which entity (table) within the CRM am I affecting?

- What is the direction of travel for the data (for example, is it saved to *CRM 2* or to *CRM 1*?).

With this information, we build up a common naming convention as follows:

```
<CUD action><Entity name><Direction>
```

The logic apps were therefore named in this style:

```
CreateContactCRM1toCRM2
DeleteSalesTransacitonCRM2toCRM1
UpdateContactEmailCRM1toCRM2
```

This helps me to see immediately what each object in the resource group is intended to do.

When ready to try the logic app in the next phase of development (such as when it is ready for peer testing), we would create a copy of the logic app in the testing resource group with the same name.

Tip

To simplify searching for specific resources and to make it easier for other project members to understand the objects you have created, **metadata** can be added in the form of tags. These are key:value strings that you can create and are often used to determine other key information about your object, such as who the author was, what group it belongs to, what the direction of travel for the data is, and what the key entity being developed is.

The following screenshot shows new tags being added to this logic app:

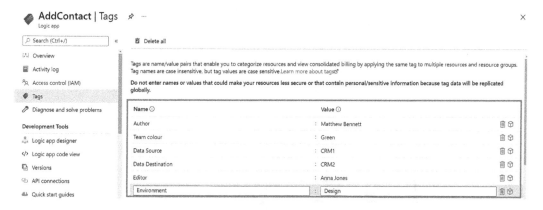

Figure 2.4 – Tags help to understand the nature and purpose of the object

As you can see from the preceding screenshot, tags are a useful way to determine which project your resource is associated with, who authored the resource, and other keywords and metrics you might want to use to search the Azure cloud. This is especially important in that as your projects grow, take on new phases, scope outward, and mature over time, the number of resources you will host will build up, making the management of your resources an essential skill.

Let's look at how to create a resource group.

Exercise – creating a resource group

Follow these instructions to create a resource group:

1. From the home page, select the **Resource groups** button:

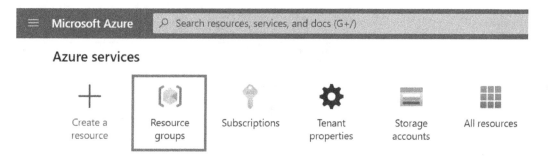

Figure 2.5 – The Resource groups button

This may seem a little strange, but if you use the **Create a resource** button, you will be presented with the object catalog.

2. On the **Resource groups** overview page, press the **Add** button:

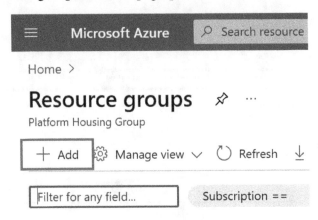

Figure 2.6 – Pressing the Add button

3. On the **Create a resource group** form, ensure that you are paying for this resource by using your *MSDN subscription*, not **Pay as you go**. Enter a name for the resource group and select the region where you would like to store this resource group. Here, **UK West** is chosen:

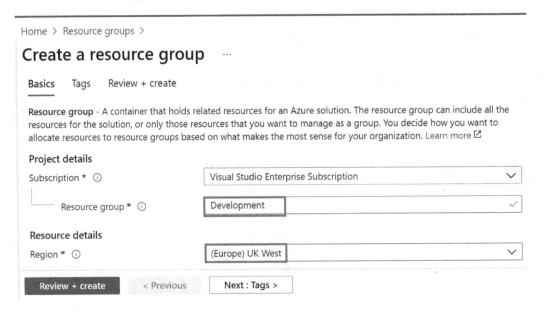

Figure 2.7 – Creating the resource group, page 1

4. (Optional but recommended) Add tags to explain the nature and purpose of the new resource group (this can be done later once the resource group has been created):

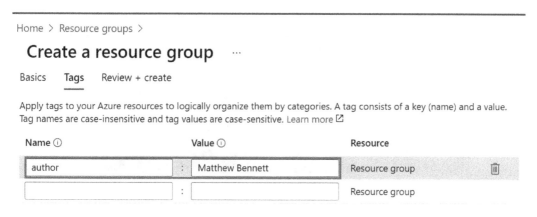

Figure 2.8 – Tagging the resource group

5. (Optional) Press **Review + create**. A summary of the creation request will be presented to you as shown in this screenshot:

Home > Resource groups >

Create a resource group   ...

✅ Validation passed.

Basics   Tags   **Review + create**

Basics

Subscription	Visual Studio Enterprise Subscription
Resource group	Development
Region	UK West

Tags

author	Matthew Bennett

Create   < Previous   Next >   Download a template for automation

Figure 2.9 – Review + create summary

6. As mentioned earlier, tagging, and checking the summary page are optional. If you know what you are doing, you can press **Create** on the initial page. Press **Create** to create the resource group.

Once created, you will get a pop-up message to inform you that the resource group has been created. You can navigate directly to the new resource group using the buttons on the popup; however, the message is only present for a few seconds:

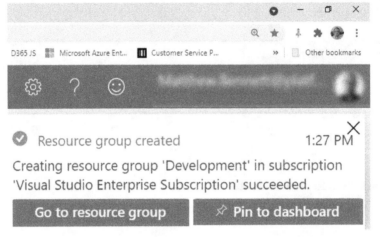

Figure 2.10 – The resource group created pop-up message

Go to resource group will take you directly to the **Overview** page for the new resource group:

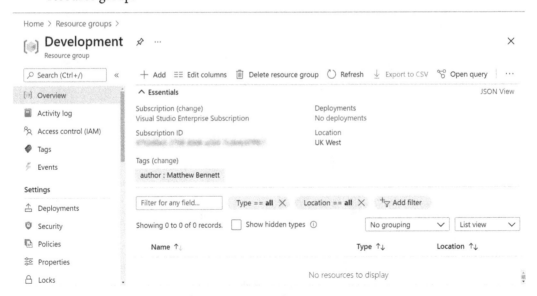

Figure 2.11 – The Overview page for your new resource group

If you plan to use this resource on a regular basis, it would be a good idea to pin it to the dashboard so you can directly access this resource group with fewer mouse clicks.

7. If you miss the pop-up message, you can see the new resource group by navigating to the **Resource groups** section as before, and it will appear in the list of available resource groups linked to your subscription:

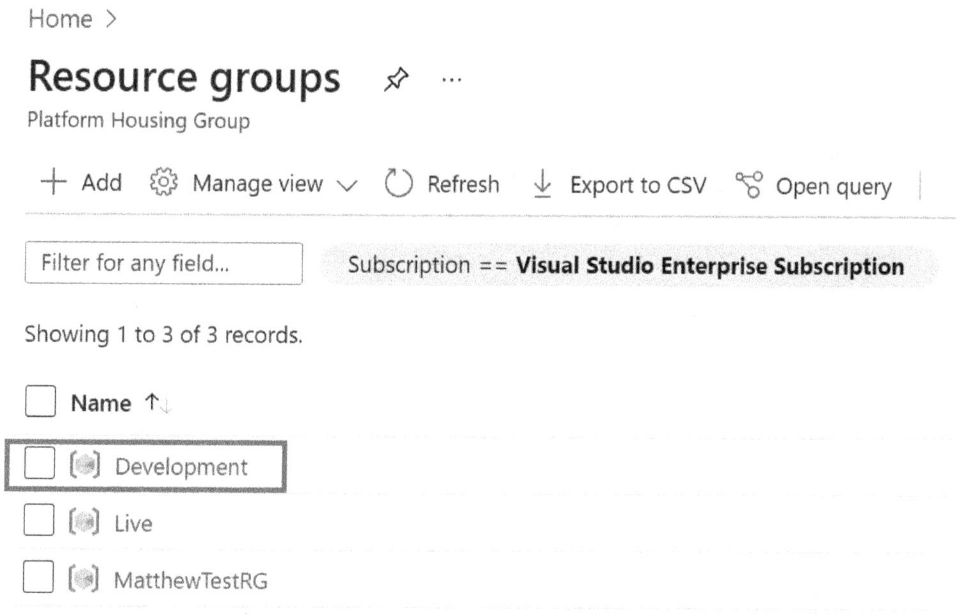

Home >

Resource groups ✈ ···
Platform Housing Group

╋ Add   ⚙ Manage view ∨   ◯ Refresh   ↓ Export to CSV   ⚇ Open query

| Filter for any field... | Subscription == **Visual Studio Enterprise Subscription** |

Showing 1 to 3 of 3 records.

☐ **Name** ↑↓

☐ [●] Development

☐ [●] Live

☐ [●] MatthewTestRG

Figure 2.12 – The Resource groups page listing your new resource group

In this exercise, you have created a new resource group. You have considered the logical design for your Azure environment. You have also considered that some resources are unique in that they can only be named once (such as is the case with Azure functions). However, most resources such as logic apps can exist with the same name but are partitioned by placing them into different resource groups.

So over time, your resource group will fill with resources. You might need to consider breaking them up into other, smaller, more manageable resource groups as the project unfolds.

Moving resources

We have already started to cover this in the preceding exercise. Once created, resources can be renamed, or a clone of the resource can be created, but it must exist within the same resource group. If you want to do this, the new copy will need to have a different name.

To move a resource between resource groups, you need to manually create a new instance in the new resource group and then copy the code across to the new version in the new resource group.

When creating a copy of an existing logic app for a new resource group (such as adding it to the test resource group), you might consider using the **Clone** button located on the **Overview** page for that resource. However, cloning will create a second copy within the same resource group, which is not what you are trying to achieve. The name of the clone will also need to be different as you cannot have two copies of a resource with the same name in a resource group.

The better option is to create a new blank logic app in the test environment and then copy the JSON code from the old logic app to replace that of the new logic app.

Remember that any Common Data Service actions in the testing version of the logic app will need to be amended to point to the test environment, not the development environment.

Exercise – creating a copy in another resource group

We are going to look at how we can move a resource. This is quite tricky as in most cases, a resource is tied to its resource group on its creation. logic apps can be cloned within a resource group and functions are often re-deployed using Visual Studio. One sure-fire way is to copy a logic app's JSON code and then manually update the environment settings as in the following steps:

1. From the old resource group, navigate to the **Overview** page of the resource. Make a note of the exact spelling of the logic app.

2. Open the resource in code view by pressing **logic app code view**:

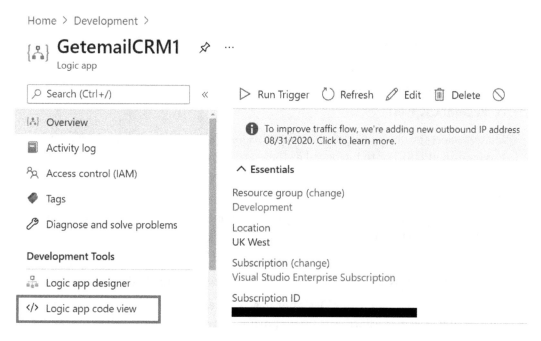

Figure 2.13 – Opening in code view

3. Copy all the code to the clipboard, or to Notepad.

4. Navigate to the new resource group. On the resource group overview page for the **Testing** resource group, press the **Add** button to add a new resource.

5. In the search field, type `logic app`.

6. Select the traditional logic app (first in the list).

7. You will be presented with the details page explaining what a logic app is. Press **Create** to continue with the wizard:

Figure 2.14 – Logic App catalog page

Create the logic app with the following parameters:

A. **Subscription: Visual Studio Enterprise Subscription (MSDN account)**

B. **Resource group: Testing**

C. **Logic App name**: GetemailCRM1

D. **Region: UK West**

Do not select the checkboxes to associate this logic app with an **Integration Service Environment** (**ISE**) or to be logged as these are not necessary at this time. We will discuss what these items do in *Chapter 3*, *Referencing Data within Actions* – review the *Logic app creation* exercise.

8. (Optional) If you wish to do so at this juncture, you can tag the logic app, but this can be done at a later stage.

9. Press **Review + create**. The logic app will be created.

10. On the pop-up message, navigate directly to the newly created logic app.

11. You will be on the **Logic Apps Designer** page where you are being presented with a series of templates to start your development. As we have code ready to use, select **Blank Logic App**.

12. You are presented with a blank logic app in the Designer window and are presented with trigger options. Press the **Code view** button:

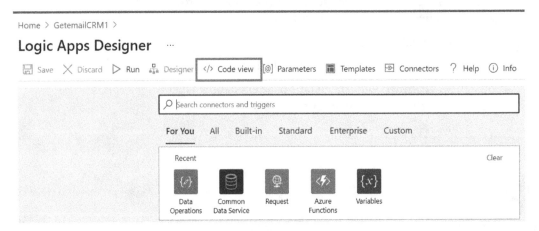

Figure 2.15 – Pressing the Code view button

13. Replace the existing JSON code with the code from the old version of the logic app. Press **Save** when you are ready:

```
1   {
2       "definition": {
3           "$schema": "https://schema.management.azure.com/providers/Microsoft.Logic/schemas/2016-06-01/workflowdefinition.json#",
4           "actions": {
5               "Get_record": {
6                   "inputs": {
7                       "host": {
8                           "connection": {
9                               "name": "@parameters('$connections')['commondataservice']['connectionId']"
10                          }
11                      },
12                      "method": "get",
13                      "path": "/v2/datasets/@{encodeURIComponent(encodeURIComponent('          crm11'))}/tables/@{encodeURIComponent
14                  },
15                  "runAfter": {},
16                  "type": "ApiConnection"
17              },
```

Figure 2.16 – Saving the code from the old logic app

14. Press the **Designer** button to return to the frontend designer.

15. Amend any Common Data Service actions in your logic app to instead point to the **Testing** environment:

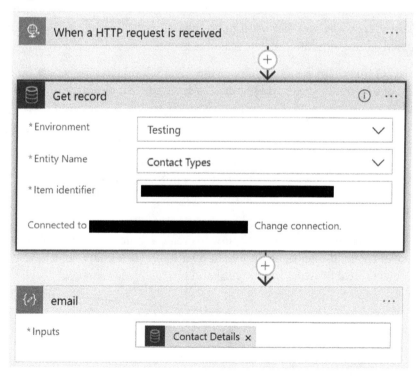

Figure 2.17 – The Common Data Service action is now pointing to
the testing version of the CRM environment

The Common Data Service is now pointing to the **Testing** environment as in the preceding screenshot.

> **Note**
>
> As the logic app is new, the trigger URL will have been randomly generated and will be different from the URL used in the old logic app. Please ensure to update any web APIs you have that need to point to this version of the logic app.

So, while not strictly a move of the same resource, the resource can at least be copied to a new resource group using this method. The old version of the resource can be disabled or deleted if no longer required.

Summary

In this chapter, we have looked at the concept of the resource group as a logical container of resources. We have looked at some resources that are unique within the tenant, some of which can have the same name but be in different resource groups. We have also strategically considered why you may want to do this. We have then created a resource group and copied a logic app into the new resource group.

One of the goals of this chapter was to manage the Azure cloud tenant – where we focused on the concept of a resource group and planned to structure our cloud objects into logical groupings called resource groups. Furthermore, in the *Creating resource groups* section, we discussed how we can have copies of the same resource (such as one logic app) in different resource groups to cater to different environments (such as live, testing, and development). We also looked at the fact that function names are unique across the tenant and deployment is often to a specific resource group where it can be used centrally. If we want to move a function, the most common method is to delete it and to re-deploy from Visual Studio.

In the next chapter, we are going to look at how to create a logic app and work with variables. We will create, initialize, and populate a variable, read JSON objects, and reference an object's field by using both logical and physical field names.

3
Referencing Data within Actions

In this chapter, we are going to look at the **Declare, Instantiate, Populate (DIP)** process in action and how you can make your own variables, set data, and manipulate data as the logic app run proceeds.

We will take a deeper look at JSON messages, which are the staple for sending data universally. Finally, we will also consider how data is stored and structured by applications and their underlying databases by accessing data using logical as well as physical field names.

At the end of this chapter, you will be able to use variables as well as read data stored in complex objects and pass them into an external system or application.

In this chapter, you will learn about the following:

- Discovering how to create, initialize, populate, and use a variable
- Discovering how to read a JSON message
- Discovering how to reference a field using both logical and physical field names

The chapter covers the following main areas:

- Working with and accessing data
- How to read JSON
- Logical versus physical field names

Technical requirements

To work on this chapter, you will need the following:

- A web browser
- An Azure subscription
- A standard Azure Logic App containing a trigger of your choice to start the logic app (commonly a recurrence or HTTP request trigger)

Working with and accessing data

To work with data within a logic app, we will need to determine how to access data. As other chapters cover accessing data using triggers and more specific means, we will focus here on how to manipulate the data once you have some already at your disposal.

You are going to create a variable, call it into being, populate it with data, and then use the variable through the life of the logic app run.

Azure Logic Apps is an extremely powerful tool that will enable you to quickly (if you prefer to use the editor) manipulate common forms of data without writing code.

Getting started with variables

A variable is an object containing a label and a piece of data. It can store most types of data, but the most common for use in logic apps is the `string` data type.

Data types you can use are the following:

- **Integer**: Represents a whole number, for example, `1946`.
- **Float**: Represents a specific type of number containing a decimal point and subsequent numbers after the decimal point, for example, `3.14159265`.

- **String**: A sequence of characters. These can be a combination of numbers, symbols, alphabetic characters, and spaces. Non-visible (not parsable) characters such as regular expressions (regex, for example, /n) will be treated as characters, not as additional commands. An example of a string sequence might be an address field: `45, Larkhill Rise`.

Note that *parsing* is a process we will explain in greater detail in *Chapter 4, Reading Complex Data*.

> **Good to know**
>
> Most programming languages have special symbols used for common actions such as to indicate where a line ends. These originally stem from print PostScript languages used by early dot-matrix, daisy wheel, or LaserJet printers to know when to move the carriage to a new line. They are referred to as *regular expressions* and are often used to find the start point and end point of a line to be able to make replacements in a text file in bulk. A good tool that makes use of RegEx is Notepad++, available here: `https://notepad-plus-plus.org`.

- **Boolean**: Logic apps are quite specific in how they use Boolean operators. As the name implies, **Boolean** is a two-state logic system (two possible options: for example, 1 or 0, yes or no, on or off, up or down). With both C# and Logic Apps, a Boolean is thought of as three-state logic, that of `true`, `false`, or `null`.

> **Note**
>
> If no initial value is supplied, the inference is that the variable is initially holding `null`.

- **Array**: An array is a list of values, as one row. Think of a row of numbers, for example, the Fibonacci sequence: 1, 2, 3, 5, 8, 13, 21. These can be represented as an array of 7 values and can be referenced by using their position in the array, where the first number is stored at position 0.

Arrays are written in the JSON language as a JSON message, and the array is encapsulated in square brackets to define the set of values in an array. To write two rows of equal size (for example, the first five numbers in the two- and three-times tables), two messages are held within the array, as follows:

```
[
  {
    2,4,6,8,10
  },
```

```
    {
        3,6,9,12,15
    }
  ]
```

Arrays are held as a `String` object but can be *parsed* (read by the logic app and split apart into different variables).

- **Objects**: An object is potentially a collection of values, arrays, and other data types. The object can be considered a *bag* and different data variables within the object can be accessed separately once parsed. This is a useful tool when you want to analyze a complex set of variables from the same source and then focus on just one variable or just one section, as in the following example:

```
<?xml version="1.0" ?>
<Root>
<ContactDetails query="Where the contact-ref =
&apos;375798643&apos;"/>
<ErrorDetails>No contact was found where the contact-ref
= &apos;375798643&apos;
</ErrorDetails>
</Root>
```

As you can see from the code, there is a `ContactDetails` section and an `ErrorDetails` section, which can be read separately by the logic app if required.

DIP process in action

The process of storing a variable has two parts:

1. Instantiate the variable.
2. Set the variable.

This is in line with the programming process that follows:

1. **Declaration**: Define the name of the object that will store the value, and the type of data you wish to store.
2. **Instantiation**: Call the object into being in readiness to store the value. In low-level programming languages that would require the allocation of memory to hold the value at a specific address location in machine code.
3. **Population**: Add the actual value to be stored.

Within logic apps, this is a two-stage process (although it is possible to do all three stages in one action).

Initializing the variable

The **Initialize variable** action is placed at the very beginning of the logic app, immediately following the trigger action that starts the logic app run. It is made up of three sections:

- **Name**: This is the name of the variable you want to use to call the data.
- **Type**: This is the type of data you wish to store (the default is **String**).
- **Value**: Fill this in if the data is already known at the start of the logic app run, or the data is constant (it is not going to change, for example, in mathematics, pi is 3.14159265).

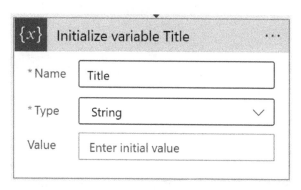

Figure 3.1 – Initializing a variable

So, in the preceding figure, we have declared Title and set its expected data type to hold text (**String**). However, the variable is currently empty, or as we would say, its default data is currently in use as the variable is holding null.

To null or not to null

Null is a very strange and confusing item that confuses many a programmer. Null refers to the variable being empty, and to all intents and purposes, null does mean empty, however, strictly speaking, null is a value. Null is an integer meaning *nothing is there*, but it is not zero. Zero can be calculated. When I have the sum *2-2*, I get zero because I am numerically reducing on a scale. Null sits apart from zero and is thought of more as a character that represents an empty void.

JSON code view – Initialize variable Title

If you are comfortable working in the code editor, the JSON code for this action
is as follows:

```
"Initialize_variable_Title": {          #Line 1
            "inputs": {                 #Line 2
            "variables": [
                    {
                            "name": "Title",
                            "type": "string"
                    }
            ]
        },
        "runAfter": {          #Line 10
            "Initialize_variable_ID": [
                "Succeeded"
            ]
        },
        "type": "InitializeVariable"
    }
```

Let's look at the structure of this action:

On line 1, the highlighted text is the action name. This can be renamed at this point,
however, be mindful of the fact that this action is followed by a successive action, which
will have a runAfter section. If you do change the action title, please remember to also
update the runAfter section to the successive action.

Line 2 contains the data schema. This is the structure of the object and is used to define
what is being stored and how we can access it. In this example, this is a simple variable
storing one value with a name of Title and a data type of String.

On line 10, we have the runAfter section. This is used by Azure to understand where to
place the action in the logic app's structure.

> **Did you know?**
>
> For logic apps, it appears that the JSON code structure of the logic app file is back to front! The JSON file header explains the connection objects used within the logic app. The **Action** section has the action at the bottom of the logic app as the first action in the JSON code. Given the fact that variable instantiations are at the top of the logic app, they will appear at the very bottom of the **Action** section when reading the JSON code.

Finally, line 15 defines what the action object is. In this case, the action is to initialize the variable.

Setting the variable

Quite often, data will not be revealed to you immediately at the start of the logic app run or may need to be calculated or retrieved further down in the logic app run. Here, we store the data value as it currently stands at that point in time by using the **Set variable** action.

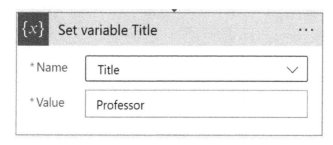

Figure 3.2 – Setting the variable with data

The **Set variable** action is often used within a `ForEach` branch as different data values are used to temporarily store data specific to that record.

For example, I want to add 10 people from a database to a CRM enterprise system such as *Salesforce*. I have a SQL **Get rows** action that obtains the 10 records from the database table. This is then followed by a **ForEach** action, which performs data manipulation and finally creates a new record in the CRM system.

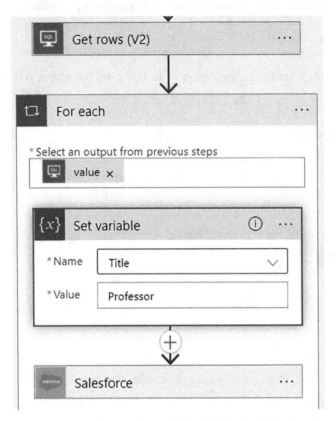

Figure 3.3 – Setting the variable with a hardcoded value

Can you see something wrong with this section?

Yes – **Title** is hardcoded as `Professor`. This will add all 10 people into Salesforce with the title of *Professor*, when they might not be!

To fix this, we can take the field from the available fields from a SQL table as there is a **List Records/Get record** action already called. As this is a customer record and we know that we have stored a **Title** field, we should replace `Professor` and in the **Value** field, instead add dynamic content by selecting from the selector **Title**.

In the following example, I have used Dynamics 365 as my source, rather than a SQL database, but the principle is the same:

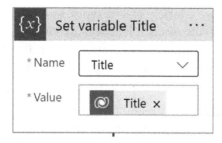

Figure 3.4 – Setting Title with a dynamic title from Dynamics 365

Notice that the value being set is the found **title** for this contact, rather than hardcoding every new contact as `Professor`.

How to read JSON

We've already started to explore how to work with JSON and covered some of the basics of the language, but let's revisit this.

JavaScript Object Notation (JSON) is the common language used for storing and exchanging data and replaces the earlier language **Extensible Markup Language (XML)**, which is still used by some older systems.

One key difference is that JSON is JavaScript. JavaScript was designed to run on the client browser, to enhance the experience for the user further than what could be achieved with HTML alone.

JSON is written in readable *English* text but has a clearly defined structure. There are a few rules when working with data for which JSON was deliberately designed:

- When you communicate between the client and server, the data should only be text. Modern dynamic web pages are rendered on the server and a copy of the HTML is sent to the client. This makes it difficult for hackers to determine the names of database or web page fields. By hiding away the field names and sending only text across, this obfuscation increases security.

- Any JavaScript object or function we create can communicate with the server using text.

- Any return data from the server is also text and as such can be used within functions, client-side.

- As we are using text, there is little parsing or data manipulation needed.

That said, enterprise systems use a variety of data types, so it is important to know what data is stored within the entity (the record). Just because JSON uses text (`string`) as the default, does not mean that the enterprise system you are creating or updating a record on expects the same. Some data conversions will still be needed, and this is one of the main jobs of a logic app.

This example uses the JavaScript `stringify` function to parameterize (parse) the JSON object and create a sentence that will pop up as an alert message:

```
<!DOCTYPE html>
<html>
<body>
<h2>This script will use the Stringify JavaScript function to
parse my object.</h2>
<script>
var theObject = { name: "Matthew", age: 44, city: "Mansfield"
};
var JSONcode = JSON.stringify(theObject);
window.location = "welcometoJSON.php?x=" + JSONcode;
</script>
</body>
</html>
```

Here, the JavaScript uses a JSON action to read the string stored in the variable and turns it into a sentence by using the **Stringify** action, which parses the values stored in the JSON message output each one found:

```
Matthew from Mansfield is 44
```

The basic message is encapsulated by using curly brackets (also known as curly braces), which form the start and end of the message. The message is split using a key-value pair combination. The first word is the name of the variable that will hold the value and the second is the data value itself.

> **Tip**
>
> To help you to read JSON quickly, logic app JSON code is color-coded in red
> for the variable name and blue for the actual data, or in the case of dynamic
> data, the location where the data can be found.

JSON code view – Set variable Title

If you use the code editor, the JSON code for the static variable at the top of this section is
as follows:

```
"Set_variable_Title": {#Line 1
            "inputs": {#Line 2
                "name": "Title",
                "value": "Professor"
            },
            "runAfter": {#Line 6
                "Compose_to_check_for_empty_record_set": [
                    "Succeeded"
                ]
            },
            "type": "SetVariable"
        }
```

On line 1, we set the action title. Again, if you have a succeeding action, the `runAfter`
section on that action will also need to be updated.

On line 2, we see not the data schema but this time the actual value to be stored. This is
presented as a key-value pair, which is a common building block of JSON coding:

```
{
    "name": "Title",
    "value": "Professor"
}
```

In English, this would simply be: *The title is Professor*.

In a high-level programming language such as BASIC, you might write this as follows:

```
10 LET title = "Professor"
```

But back to our JSON block, on line 6, the `runAfter` section defines where the action is to be performed in the logic app structure.

Finally, `type` refers to the type of action we are performing.

Exercise

Aim: Create a minimal logic app to extract the output of a JSON message sent to this logic app.

Sometimes I like to look at a logic app run and try to determine what data was captured and confirm whether this data is correct. Our starting point is often a JSON message sent either by an external system or by another logic app. This message's data will be *dynamic* in nature, so you might expect to see different data for each message received. In this case, we have the most minimal logic app of one trigger and one action, which outputs the body of the message.

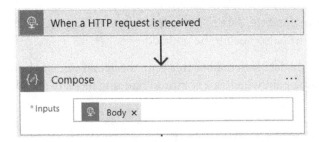

Figure 3.5 – The Compose action will store the body of the message

To create this, do the following:

1. Create a new logic app as explained in *Chapter 2, Environments and Resource Groups*.

2. You will be presented with a welcome screen where you can start with an existing template or are prompted to select from a choice of common triggers. Select a *blank template*. (Alternatively, select the HTTP trigger – option 2 in the screenshot which will do this part for you):

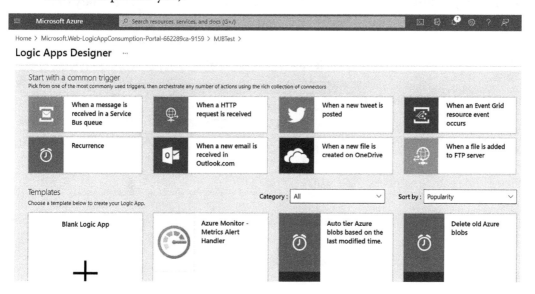

Figure 3.6 – Getting started by selecting from the catalog of templates and triggers

3. For your choice of trigger, select an HTTP request.

4. In the request body, add the schema for the JSON message you are expecting to receive. This is so that the message can be parsed.

> **Tip**
> If you don't know the message structure or expect that the message may be different each time you receive one, use empty curly brackets. The message will be received but not parsed and the logic app will be able to continue.

5. After the trigger, insert a new action and from the catalog, select **Data Operations | Compose**.

6. In the **Compose** input field, from the **Dynamic content** menu, select **Body** from the previous action.

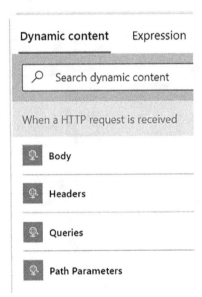

Figure 3.7 – Selecting Dynamic content from the variable catalog

7. Run the logic app, either by sending data from another logic app or via a Postman call to the URL of the trigger.

Your message will appear in the **Compose** action.

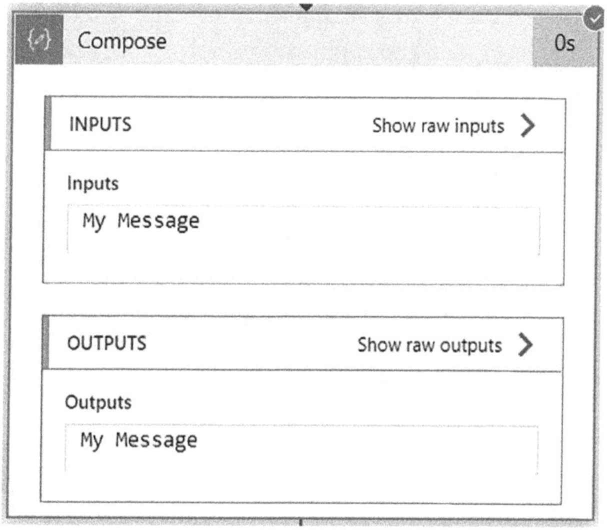

Figure 3.8 – Logic app run in Data view, showing My Message as the stored value

As a result of this, we have been able to create a logic app that we can start either manually or via a POST JSON message, which will set the text My Message on the **Compose** action. The **Compose** action can be treated like a temporary variable and is often used for calculating or manipulating data as the logic app proceeds through its actions.

What is parsing?

Parsing is the process of breaking down an object or a JSON message into its component parts. For example, in the case of *James from Stevenage who is 27*, this would parse to the following:

- James
- Stevenage
- 27

If you do not parse the message, the entire message will be read as a string, which is not useful.

Logical versus physical field names

Let's take a moment to think about how *web applications* work. They are a two-tier system containing a database (low level) and the application (high level). The user interfaces with web forms, which, when combined, form the enterprise system. The forms contain fields, and these fields are named.

A user does not have the ability to see the form field names. They see text labels next to the field that contains the data. If you were to use Google Chrome's inspector or an extension such as *Level up*, you could obtain the field names used on the form.

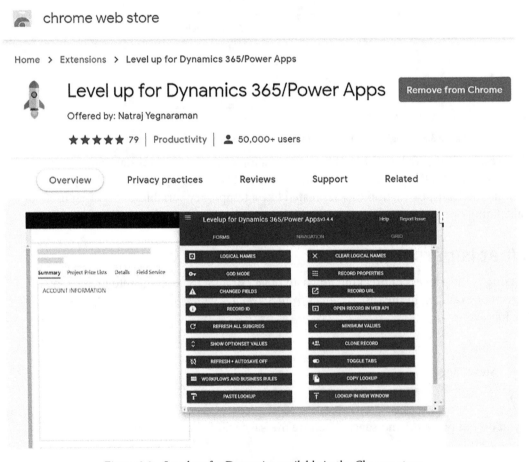

Figure 3.9 – Level up for Dynamics available in the Chrome store

The direct URL to download *Level up* is https://chrome.google. com/webstore/detail/level-up-for-dynamics-365/ bjnkkhimoaclnddigpphpgkfgeggokam?hl=en.

The data that is surfaced by the fields on the frontend form is stored in a table in a database. These attributes (fields) are named separately, and the field names of the database are often deliberately different from those of the form fields (for example, please refer to the following screenshot):

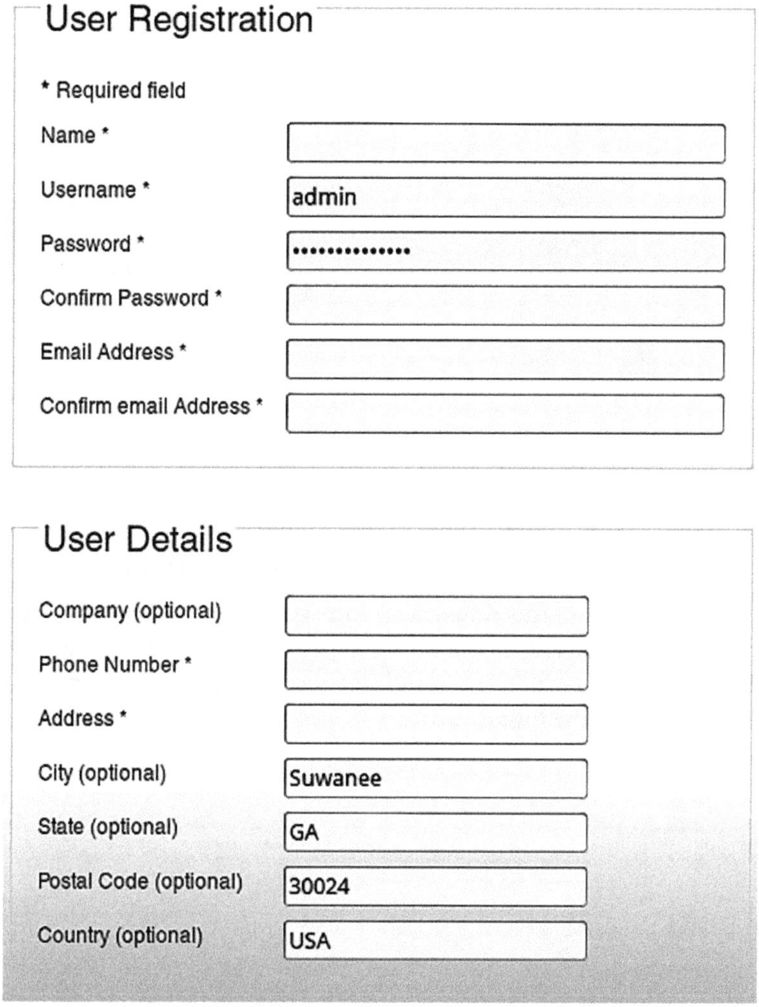

User Registration

* Required field

Name *

Username *   admin

Password *   ••••••••••••••

Confirm Password *

Email Address *

Confirm email Address *

User Details

Company (optional)

Phone Number *

Address *

City (optional)   Suwanee

State (optional)   GA

Postal Code (optional) 30024

Country (optional)   USA

Figure 3.10 – A Dynamics 365 user registration form

It is commonplace to use the Power Apps tool at make.powerapps.com to create a Power Apps table. This will list the physical names (database field names) used when we access a record directly from the SQL database, or via Common Data Service. It will also show the logical names that are used by the enterprise application system and are the names you see when selecting variables from **Dynamic catalog** in a logic app.

For now, the main point is that database fields access data from the database level to the application level. Common Data Service and *Dynamics 365/Zendesk/Salesforce* or any other application access data using the application-level field name.

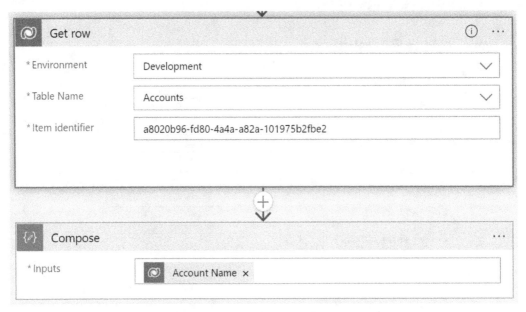

Figure 3.11 – Obtaining and storing the account name from a given Dynamics 365 account

The preceding screenshot shows this rather well – the item identifier is the logical name within Common Data Service. We are obtaining a specific record where the record ID (known as a GUID) has been hardcoded in the **Get record** action. Account Name is the logical name of a variable on the found record.

Summary

In this chapter, we looked at specific ways you can access and store data within a logic app. We looked at the concept of a variable, which is commonly used to store a specific data type (a unit of data). This could be static in nature, meaning that the number is fixed through the life of the logic app run, or may be updated at different stages within the logic app run.

We also looked at an array – a set of values of the same data type – and mentioned an object, which can store multiple fields, all of which may be different data types.

We saw the DIP process in action and two different ways to set data within a logic app run. We were able to initialize a variable, then later set a variable at the point that it was needed. We also learned how to read JSON and understood that JSON is the underlying language used not only to read data by logic apps but also that a logic app itself is created and coded using JSON. We looked at the process of breaking down an object into its component parts and accessing these separately – a process known as parsing.

Finally, we considered accessing data in the application and the difference between a field in the database storing data and a field on a form in the application, which will likely have a different field name (as well as a label on the form) from the database field it accesses. Having read this chapter, you can confidently work with data within JSON and within a logic app.

In the next chapter, we will discover how to read a JSON message and manipulate it, extract data from specific fields within a SQL output or a JSON message and use XPath to extract data from an XML message.

4
Reading Complex Data

Working with basic variables is a good start, but the power of a logic app comes with its ability to read, parameterize, and work with different types of data formats at the same time. You may also need to pass several hundred messages at the same time through your logic app.

Take, for example, the use of a logic app to transfer contacts from one system to another. You may need to work in bulk and process several hundred at a time. This chapter looks at how you can easily add this degree of power to your logic app.

In this chapter, we're going to cover the following topics:

- Accessing and parsing a JSON array
- Parsing output from a SQL query output
- Using XPath to parse an XML array

By the end of this chapter, you will be able to do the following:

- Read a JSON message and manipulate it.

- Extract data from specific fields within a SQL output, or a JSON message.

- Use XPath to extract data from an XML message.

Technical requirements

In addition to the technical requirements stated in earlier chapters, here you might like to reference the following online resources:

- **JSON Lint** (`https://jsonlint.com`): This is one of many JSON online validators that will not only check your code for errors but also prettify the code, indenting it into a normal JSON structure.

- **JSON Formatter** (`https://jsonformatter.org`): This is also a very useful online site that will format, beautify, and minify your code, should you need to store it all on one line. The site will also convert your JSON code to CSV, YAML, and XML formats.

- **JSON Schema tool** (`https://jsonschema.net/home`): This is a great site for generating a JSON schema file, which explains the structure of your JSON message. The schema generated is a full, formal schema, so there are quite a lot of elements you don't need, but if you are interested in all the possible options that could be stored in the message, this is a good place to check your code.

- **W3Schools SQL course** (`https://www.w3schools.com/sql`): Whether you are a newbie or a pro, this series of wiki pages is my favorite reference tool. SQL is quite an easy language for querying your database, but if you don't use it every day, you might like to use this site to remind you of key SQL terms. This is extremely useful because there are built-in *Try it for yourself* tools where you can experience the SQL code and test your learning.

- Unsure about XPath? Use **Codebeautify's XPath Tester** (`https://codebeautify.org/Xpath-Tester`): This invaluable tool will show you sample XML, allow you to create a path to obtain a section of data from the XML message, and it also contains example paths to get you started, allowing you to apply the same to your own XML code and test it before using in the logic app.

- **OData site** (`https://www.odata.org/`): I find this site to be helpful, especially if I need a greater understanding of OData as a general language.

- **OData query reference**: Most of the time, I need to reference OData resources to help me get my syntax correct when creating OData database queries. The Nintex Hawkeye OData guide is an invaluable reference for the correct spelling of operators and contains plenty of query examples: `https://help.nintex.com/en-US/xtensions/03_Advanced/02_Extensions/PRC_05EXT_query_builder.htm`.

- Knowledge of XML and SQL queries is also required.

Accessing and parsing a JSON array

A JSON array is used to store a sequence of data of the same type. This may be a string of numbers or text, for example:

```
[2,4,6,8,10]
```

Alternatively, it may look like this:

```
["John Smith", "Robert Lowe", "Victor Fisher", "Sarah Sutton",
"Julie Evans"]
```

The problem here is that you have a set of data and in the case of the names above, each of these may be the name of a contact you wish to add to your enterprise system. To do this, you need to take each name in turn and perform the same action (the act of creating a contact and adding the name into it). To do this, we use the **ForEach** loop to process each name separately.

However, there is a problem.

When the logic app reads the array variable that stores the whole array, such as if we named the logic app variable `myArray`, the entire array is presented, not each component name. To clarify this, we see all the names presented as one item, rather than just John Smith. We resolve this problem by first parsing the array and then sending each separate output via a **ForEach** loop.

> **Worth noting**
>
> **Parse** is a technical term that means that the computer will read through a passage of text, or block of data, and split the words apart. Where a schema (a structure) has been provided, then each data element found is stored as a particular object. In the preceding example, I can parse the list of names as a variable called `Full Name`, which is designed to store data of the `string` type. This will instead ensure that five names are stored separately using the `Full Name` variable, rather than one object.

Exercise – Parsing and cycling through an array

Let's look at this in action. In this exercise, we are going to create an array and parse it to access the different elements of the array. We will then access the data for each name in turn and process it. To do this, please follow these steps:

1. As in the previous chapter, create a blank logic app with an HTTP Request trigger. Set the schema of the trigger to be { }:

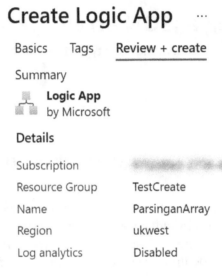

Create Logic App ⋯

Basics   Tags   **Review + create**

Summary

Logic App
by Microsoft

Details

Subscription	
Resource Group	TestCreate
Name	ParsinganArray
Region	ukwest
Log analytics	Disabled

Figure 4.1 – Creating a new logic app called ParsinganArray

Now, let's see how to create a trigger.

Creating the trigger

The very first action is to create a trigger that determines how the logic app is started. All logic apps can be run manually, but usually start automatically upon an event. Here, we are going to start the logic app if I send a **POST** message to it or can still start the logic app manually.

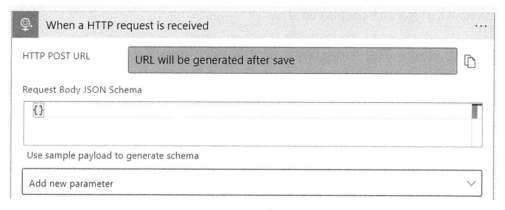

Figure 4.2 – Creating a request trigger with a blank schema

> **Tip**
>
> Why do I prefer to use HTTP Request triggers in my logic apps? There are many ways to trigger a logic app, but some are more efficient than others. As I am not waiting for the system to pass data through into the logic app, I can trigger it either manually or by sending a **POST** message via a Postman call, which gives me the option to send data I may want to use.
>
> Another alternative if you do want the logic app to repeat on a schedule is to use the **Recurrence** action; however, I have created logic apps and left them enabled in development only to find that they ran unnecessarily (incurring costs).

Follow these steps to create a trigger:

1. Initialize a variable and set it to the data type of **Array**. I am going to call this variable myArray.

2. In the same action, add the data to store for this array:

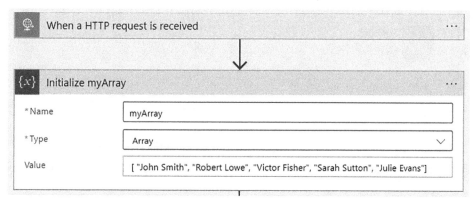

Figure 4.3 – Trigger followed by the populated myArray array

We now have a trigger and a populated array.

JSON code view – The myArray variable with populated data

This is how the `Initialize_myArray` action looks in code view:

```
"Initialize_myArray": {
            "runAfter": {},
            "type": "InitializeVariable",
            "inputs": {
                "variables": [
                    {
                        "name": "myArray",
                        "type": "array",
                        "value": "["John Smith", "Robert
Lowe", "Victor Fisher", "Sarah Sutton", "Julie Evans"]"
                    }
                ]
            }
        }
```

1. Next, we are going to add a **ForEach** action, which will read the separate names and process them individually. Select the **For each** action from the Dynamic catalog:

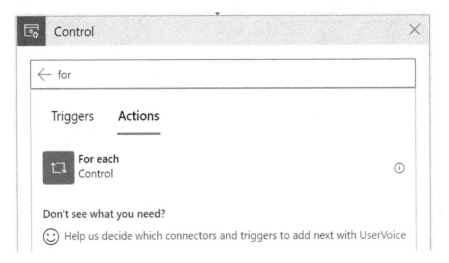

Figure 4.4 – Searching for the For each Control action in the Dynamic catalog

Once you have selected the **For each** control, we can populate it to link it to the array.

2.   Create a **ForEach** loop and set the loop to use the value being parsed from the array:

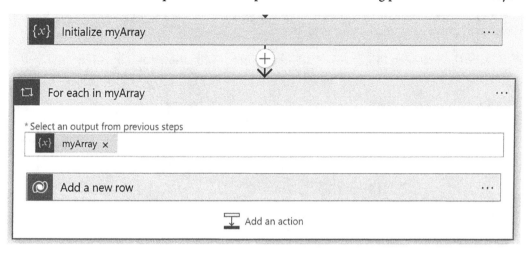

Figure 4.5 – Creating a ForEach action and referencing the array

By linking the output of the myArray variable, **ForEach** will count the number of elements in the array and process these at the same time (in parallel).

JSON code view – The ForEach action

This is the JSON code for the **ForEach** action:

```
"For_each_in_myArray": {
            "actions": {},
            "foreach": "@body('List_records')?['value']",
            "runAfter": {
                "List_records": [
                    "Succeeded"
                ]
            },
            "type": "Foreach"
        },
```

Now that you have the array being read as separate loops, we need to add each name to our new system as a new contact. For this, we are going to use the Common Data Service/ **Dataverse** to create new records for each person:

1. Inside the **For each** loop, press **Add an action** to **Add a new row**. Search for the action and click in the result list to create a new record:

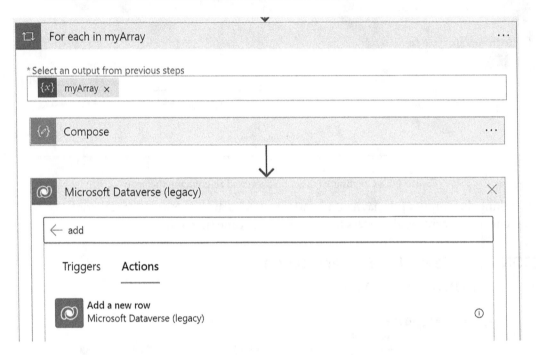

Figure 4.6 – Searching for 'Add a new row'

You now have an empty **Create** action inside the **For each** section.

2. Set the **Environment**, **Scope**, and **Entity** fields that you wish to create. Add the new parameter from the list of fields available from within the entity. In this case, we will be adding **fullname**:

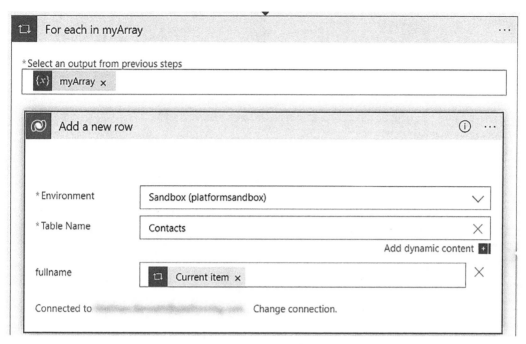

Figure 4.7 – Creating a new contact record for every contact in the array

Now that you have added an action, when the logic app is run, the array will be separated into five full names, which will then be created on the new system as five contacts. The five are processed in parallel, so the execution time will be extremely fast.

JSON code view – For each in myArray containing the Create a new record action

Here, I have provided the complete code for this section of the logic app:

```
"For_each_in_myArray": {
                "foreach": "@body('List_records')?['value']",
                "actions": {
                    "Create_a_new_record": {
                        "runAfter": {},
                        "type": "ApiConnection",
                        "inputs": {
                            "body": {
                                "crimson_systemname":
143570000,
                                "fullname": "@items('For_each_
in_myArray')",
                                "lastname": "@{body('List_
```

```
records')?['value']}",
                                    "new_contacttype": 143570001
                  },
                  "host": {
                      "connection": {
                          "name": "@
parameters('$connections')['commondataservice']
['connectionId']"
                      }
                  },
                  "method": "post",
                  "path": "/v2/datasets/@
{encodeURIComponent(encodeURIComponent('org539840ba.crm11'))}/
tables/@{encodeURIComponent(encodeURIComponent('contacts'))}/
items"
                  }
              }
          },
          "runAfter": {
              "List_records": [
                  "Succeeded"
              ]
          },
          "type": "Foreach"
      },
```

As a result of this exercise, your logic app will process all five names and add them as new contacts to your enterprise system.

Tip

There are two types of loops available from inside the **ForEach** action: **Sequential** and **Parallel**. The default is *Parallel*.

A parallel loop will set up virtual *branches* for each record in the array. In our example, we have five contacts to add, so there will be five runs of the loop, which will process at the same time. This method is more efficient, and the logic app will be very quick to run.

Alternatively, you can run the loop in *Series*. To achieve this, you need to access **Settings** for the **ForEach** action. Set the **Concurrency** to Off and the **degree of Parallelism** slider to 1. This means that each message will be dealt with one at a time in the order they are presented to the loop. This is very useful where you have a sequence of numbers in an array, and you must process these in the precise order they appear.

Parsing output from a SQL query output

If you do not already have a static dataset or are concerned that the data may update regularly and so you will not be able to use an array, you can use a SQL query to query the current state of the data in your old system and use the result as your dataset.

We are now going to uncover a new programming language used when querying data. Also, again think over how we send messages from system to system using a **REST API**.

SQL queries in action – Working with OData

OData, or the **Open Data Protocol**, is a commonly accepted, globally used standard language that is used to build RESTful APIs without having to worry about the technical details of setting up the API. OData lets the user worry about what they want, not how to send the message. For this reason, it is commonly used on queries, but is also found in the creation and use of functions where procedures are reusable (as is the case here in this logic app).

OData is approved by the **International Organization for Standardization (ISO)** and is a globally accepted language used on multiple systems.

Here is an example of an OData query for use on a SQL **Get Records** action:

```
d365_contactlocation eq 'SWINDON'
```

OData is specifically used when working with SQL instead of building a SQL query. If you prefer, you can create a **View**, or **Stored Procedure** and store this as part of your database and reference the **View** rather than the database table. This allows you to continue working with the SQL language and can be useful if you are unfamiliar with OData or have complex queries that are more suited to the SQL language.

Being at REST

REpresentational State Transfer (**REST**) is a style used when communicating between web-based computer systems. A server such as a SQL server, file server, applications server, or other web server, is said to be a REST-compliant, or *RESTful*, system. When the two systems talk to each other, a handshake takes place to determine if they can communicate whether the language about to be sent (the protocol) is supported and the speed at which the connection can transfer at. When this needs to be clearly defined before sending a message, the communication is said to be **stateful**. For some time, the one server will listen for a message and interpret the data stream, and then close the connection when completed. REST takes away the handshaking problem and the issues regarding communication between servers or between the client and server are no longer the issue of the user.

Exercise – Output from the SQL query

In this exercise, we are going to clone an existing logic app to make further additions to the new logic app:

1. In your earlier logic app, go to the **Overview** page. Press the **Clone** button and clone with a memorable name (I am going to call mine `Ch4ex2_SQLQuery`):

Figure 4.8 – Cloning an existing logic app

2. Edit your new logic app. Remove the **value** reference on the **ForEach** loop and remove the **Initialize variable** action.

This is what the logic app will look like now that the variable has been removed. Notice that you are prompted for a new output as this is required for the **ForEach** action to work:

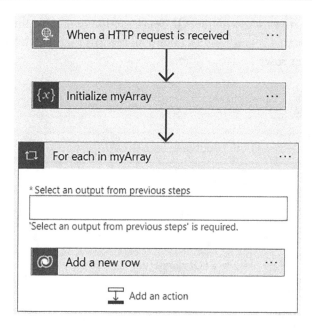

Figure 4.9 – A logic app with the previous array removed. Note the error message

At the point where the **Initialize variable** action was (in the preceding screenshot, we see an arrow, and when you hover over the arrow, the plus button will appear, allowing you to insert a new step at this point), we are going to add a replacement action:

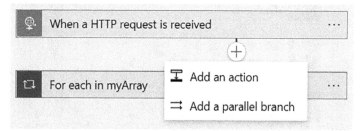

Figure 4.10 – Adding a preceding new action

3. Press the plus button to add a new action at this point. Select from the **Get Records** catalog. From the search results, you will find a section with a dark red Common Data Service database icon. Select **List records**.

> **Note**
> The Common Data Service is an accepted standard for accessing data from enterprise systems but works at the application level. If you are connecting to a traditional SQL database, you can instead use the SQL **Get Rows** action.

This screenshot shows some of the SQL Server actions available through Azure Logic Apps. Note that if you want to obtain all records that match the criteria, the SQL option is **Get rows**:

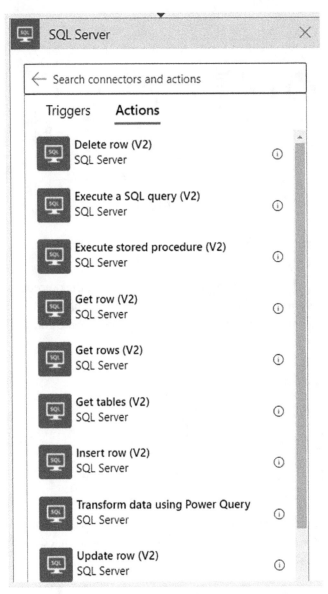

Figure 4.11 – SQL Get rows is available for traditional SQL queries

However, in the Common Data Service *actionset* equivalent, this would be **List records**. In this exercise, we will stick with the Common Data Service, which is the most common way of connecting to data on **unified enterprise systems**.

4. When adding an action in the Dynamic catalog, search for `Common Data Service`, or by *keyname* if this is already known to you. In our case, we are going to use the **List rows** action, so please search for this phrase:

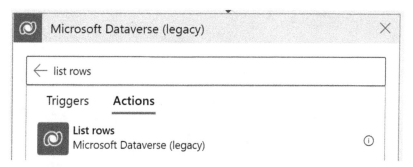

Figure 4.12 – Searching the dynamic catalog for the List rows action

5. In the new action, select **Add new parameter** and select **Filter Query**. In the **Filter Query** parameter, add an OData query to select the records you are interested in (depending on the systems you have connected your logic app to, you will need to change the entity name parameter and the data in the OData query to something more meaningful to you. However, in my example, I have a contact table where five people are based in the city of Swindon):

```
d365_contactlocation eq 'SWINDON'
```

Figure 4.13 – Adding the OData filter query

> **Tip**
>
> Remember that although we are using the Common Data Service to search both the old system and to add records to the new system, these are two separate systems.

This is the JSON code equivalent of our `List_records` action.

JSON code view – List records action

This is a JSON code for the `List_records` action:

```
"List_records": {
                "runAfter": {},
                "type": "ApiConnection",
                "inputs": {
                    "host": {
                        "connection": {
                            "name": "@
parameters('$connections')['commondataservice']
['connectionId']"
                        }
                    },
                    "method": "get",
                    "path": "/v2/datasets/@
{encodeURIComponent(encodeURIComponent('org539840ba.crm11'))}/
tables/@{encodeURIComponent(encodeURIComponent('Persons'))}/
items",
                    "queries": {
                        "$filter": "d365_contactlocation eq
'SWINDON'"
                    }
                }
            }
```

We are presuming that the old system can work with the Common Data Service and that the data is the same as the array earlier on, so we are expecting to obtain five records. Given that your table contains five records in the scope of the query, your OData query will return five records:

1. In the **ForEach** action, in the **Select an output** section, select **value** from the SQL action section in the list of dynamic variable results. This links your **ForEach** action to use the results from the OData query.

    I hope you haven't forgotten about our poor **ForEach** action? The moment we removed the `myArray` array variable, the connection to the next action was removed. This action relinks the new `List_records` action to your **ForEach** action:

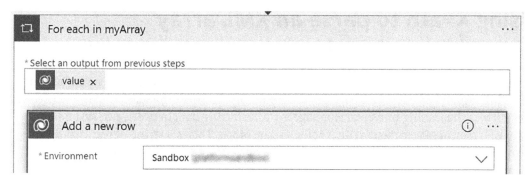

Figure 4.14 – The ForEach section refers to the found value

2. Inside the **For each** action, press the plus button to create a new action. Add a **Add a new row** action for your new system (in my case, as I am using D365, I am going to use the **Add a new row, Common Data Service** action).

3. In the new action, add the **Full Name** field. In the **Full Name** parameter, select the dynamic content field of **Full Name** from the results of your earlier OData query:

Figure 4.15 – Now, each contact will be made using each found record from the OData query

4. Save and run your logic app.

You will have successfully retrieved the five records from your SQL query and created five new contacts in your enterprise system.

Using XPath to parse an XML array

When working with static data produced from older, or *closed* systems (where it is not possible to interrogate for data using web APIs or dynamic queries), one common language is **eXtensible Markup Language** (**XML**). Originally intended to be an extension to HTML tags, it became a language on its own merits. For many years (and it is still used now), it was the leading universal language for transferring data between two systems. Early web messages were sent as an XML message block. This is a string of text that forms the object (the *record* in database terms) and the object could refer to different aspects of data.

For example, our contact in the supplying system may have basic personal details such as their title, date of birth, nationality, and the relationship the company has with this person (for example, are they a customer?):

- Attached to that data could also be an array of addresses the contact has lived at within the past 10 years.

- Attached also to the main data block could be disability details.

- Also attached could be their marketing preferences.

- Also attached could be their relationships to other contacts in the system by referencing the other persons' ID number and their association (for example, husband and wife).

The taxonomy for this example becomes the following:

```
\Root
        - Contact details
            - Address
            - Address
            - Address
            - Disability
            - Marketing
            - Relationships
```

XML is sent as a string and is parsed as text. If you are sending integers, you will need to convert from text to an integer by recomposing the value using an integer conversion function.

> **A note about date formats**
>
> Date formats are commonly stored in short-format UK date format such as dd/mm/yyyy (for example, 22/12/2016); however, modern enterprise systems typically store the date in ISO format, with yyyy-mm-dd and then the timestamp. We will discuss how to work with dates in a later chapter.

Using XPath to obtain your values

XML is an extension to HTML code and has been a common standard for sending data from one system to another. However, it has its limitations:

- Data is often saved as an XML file and is more suited for exports/imports.

- Data is stored as a string. On the original system, data may have been stored using some other data type, so data type conversion will be necessary when importing it to the new system.

- The XML file stores data in a taxonomy – a hierarchy of sections. These can be accessed in much the same way as traversing folders in Command Prompt by changing focus to the appropriate path.

As such, we use XPath to determine which folder (or section) to look at to retrieve the data values at this point. In addition, by *parsing* the XML data, we can retrieve specific variables.

In the example provided by *CodeBeautify* at `https://codebeautify.org/Xpath-Tester`, we are given a standard example that we will break down into sections to understand how the parser will read the XML message:

```
<root xmlns: foo= "http://www.foo.org/"  xmlns: bar= "http://
www.bar.org" >
    <employees>
        <employee id= "1">Jonny Dapp</employee>
        <employee id= "2">Al Pacino</employee>
        <employee id= "3">Robert De Niro</employee>
        <employee id= "4">Kevin Spacey</employee>
        <employee id= "5">Denzel Washington</employee>


    </employees>
    <foo: companies>
        <foo: company id= "6">Tata Consultancy   Services<foo:
company>

        <foo: company id= "7">Wipro</foo: company>
        <foo: company id= "8">Infosys</foo: company>
        <foo: company id= "9">Microsoft</foo: company>
        <foo: company id= "10">IBM</foo: company>
        <foo: company id= "11">Apple</foo: company>
        <foo: company id= "12">Oracle</foo: company>
    </foo: companies>
</root>
```

From this, we learn the following:

- The XML message refers to two namespaces (two systems that can read these fields).
- The source system is called `foo`.
- Any fields from the source system are prefixed with the `foo` schema (for example, `foo:company`),
- Each record has a primary key identifier called `id`.
- The `employees` section is not specific to the `foo` namespace.
- The `companies` section is specific to the `foo` namespace.

Exercise: Try it for yourself

Using the example provided on the Code Beautify site, here are some obvious navigation XPath commands I would use to filter and focus on specific data:

- To reference all the data, I would use the `root` path.
- To reference just the employees, the path is `/root/employees/employee`.
- If I want to use shorthand, the shortcut path to obtain the employees is `//employee`.
- To select all the company IDs, use `//foo:company/@id`.
- To select all IDs regardless of namespace, use `//@id`.

As you can see from this exercise, XPath can be quite easy to use to obtain data. The problem comes when your data should be an object or a set of objects. The objects contain variables of different data types, we have one array, or our object contains multiple arrays. XPath is not as sophisticated as JSON, which can be read and structured using schemas to explain what is happening at each point of the data output, so that variables, objects, and arrays can be *typed* correctly.

Summary

You are now able to add variables to your logic app to enter pre-staged data. You are also able to create arrays, which allow for powerful and quick calculations and other actions to take place on each element within your array, at the same time. You also now know two different ways to obtain dynamic data from your system – the SQL query actions and the Common Data Service actions. We have used the Common Data Service actions to obtain data and then used this to create new records on your receiving system. We also considered the use of XML instead of JSON messages where it is appropriate to do so.

In the next chapter, we are going to perform data manipulation, which is one of the key main functions of a logic app. We will perform calculations but also look at text manipulation.

5
Manipulating Data

Now that you are starting to use logic apps, we will look at more complex text and numerical data manipulations that are commonly used by developers. You will learn how to perform calculations, concatenate text, split a string, count the length of a string, and index the position of a word or character within a string.

In this chapter, you will learn how to:

- Manipulate text and numerical data
- Split complex and long strings into separate sections for further processing

In this chapter, we will cover the following main areas:

- Performing basic mathematical operations
- Combining text
- Splitting a string at a certain point
- Counting the length of a string
- Indexing the position of a character in a string

Complex manipulations

Logic apps is designed to handle data transformation in the background seamlessly and will update a system in real time, with most logic app runs taking less than a second to complete. Data can be worked on while the user is still using the system, which makes **Azure logic apps** an extension to existing and previous data transformation tools.

Language history

For Dynamics 365, and formerly in Dynamics AX and other on-premises versions, calculations were performed by creating business process workflows. These are objects that existed either as part of the entity or separate to the entity in the **Application Object Tree** (**AOT**) (this is now branded as the **Power Apps** window). Refer to the following screenshot:

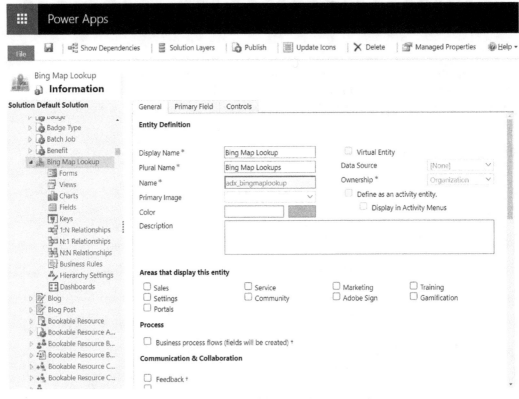

Figure 5.1 – Image of the AOT (PowerApps)

Within an entity, you have the option to make interface changes or to make decisions based on the current data values on the form. For example, you may want to show an information message at the top of the form where certain criteria are not met and then remove the message when all these criteria are met.

The other approach would be to use **X++** or **Dynamics NAV C/AL** functions. These are a series of 100 common functions not dissimilar to the functions found in Excel with which you can perform basic mathematical calculations.

Here is an example of C/AL code:

```
1 Documentation()
2 OS 102915 Object Created
3
4 OnRun()
5 IF NOT CONFIRM('Run in' + COMPANYNAME + '?') THEN
6 EXIT;
7
8 UpdateItems;
9
10 MESSAGE('Done');
```

X++ was an object-oriented language like **C#** and could be used for background calculations on web pages prior to the launch of logic apps. **X++** uses the **MorphX** development platform used to build business and accounting systems. This was found commonly in **Dynamics AX**.

The following code may look familiar to you if you are able to read **C#**. We see a list of classes and methods in a list within the editor. Here, we see the main method, which will display a message box on the screen with the text Hello World.

The **MorphX** editor is a split window with the list of functions on the left and the content of the function in the right-pane edit window.

For the main method, we simply write the following in VB/C# style code:

```
public static void main(Args args)
{
        Info("Hello World!");
}
```

Let's now move on to discuss the origins of DAX.

Origins of DAX

Data Analysis Expression (**DAX**) functions are a collection of approximately 250 mathematical, statistical, text, and manipulation functions that have been used for over thirty years and feature commonly in spreadsheet applications, notably Excel. They are commonly known as **Excel formulae**.

An example of an Excel formula is as follows:

```
=VLOOKUP(I2;$B$2:$G$9;3,FALSE)
```

In this example, I am looking for the data stored in cell I2 within a table from B2-G9. I am static referencing this table because if column I contains a series of values and I want to copy down, I2 will update to I3, and so on. However, we always want to reference the static table, which should not be updated. I am interested in the contents of the third column in the table (from left to right). FALSE refers to the fact that this is a partial match. In my example, the code 102 is looked up and it references a line describing a product called **plums** that has a color value of **yellow**.

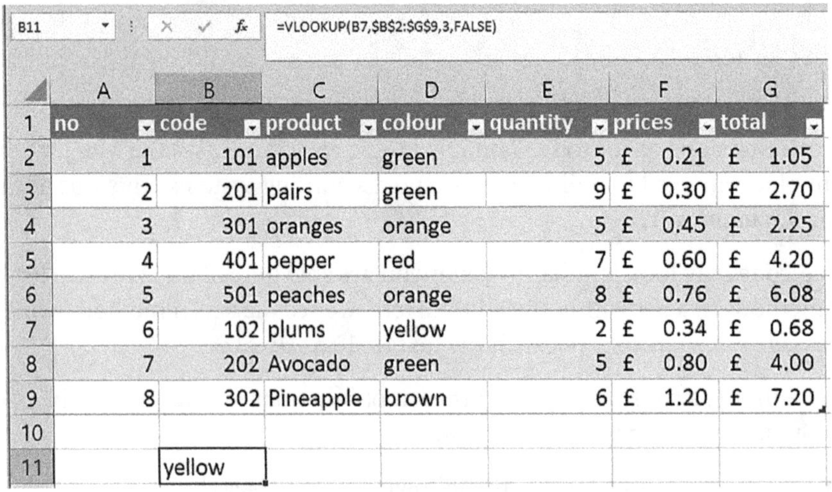

	A	B	C	D	E	F	G
		fx	=VLOOKUP(B7,$B$2:$G$9,3,FALSE)				
1	no	code	product	colour	quantity	prices	total
2	1	101	apples	green	5	£ 0.21	£ 1.05
3	2	201	pairs	green	9	£ 0.30	£ 2.70
4	3	301	oranges	orange	5	£ 0.45	£ 2.25
5	4	401	pepper	red	7	£ 0.60	£ 4.20
6	5	501	peaches	orange	8	£ 0.76	£ 6.08
7	6	102	plums	yellow	2	£ 0.34	£ 0.68
8	7	202	Avocado	green	5	£ 0.80	£ 4.00
9	8	302	Pineapple	brown	6	£ 1.20	£ 7.20
10							
11		yellow					

Figure 5.2 – Excel formula example

DAX can also be found in **Power BI** to perform data manipulation and for the visual representation of data.

If we are to consider a sum of the totals (column G in our table), this would be written in Excel as follows:

```
=SUM(G2:G9)
```

If we express this in DAX (and this is how it is used in Power BI), I would create a label (also referred to as a **measure**) to hold my Total Sales and ask that this is populated with the SUM formula. To neaten this, I have highlighted the contents of column G and created a named range called SalesAmount. Notice also that I have named the entire table Sales.

	B	C	D	E	F	G
1	no code	product	colour	quantity	prices	total
2	1 101	apples	green	8	£ 0.21	£ 1.68
3	2 201	pairs	green	7	£ 0.30	£ 2.10
4	3 301	oranges	orange	3	£ 0.45	£ 1.35
5	4 401	pepper	red	7	£ 0.60	£ 4.20
6	5 501	peaches	orange	10	£ 0.76	£ 7.60
7	6 102	plums	yellow	5	£ 0.34	£ 1.70
8	7 202	Avocado	green	6	£ 0.80	£ 4.80
9	8 302	Pineapple	brown	1	£ 1.20	£ 1.20

Figure 5.3 – Example of a SUM formula in Excel

Therefore, in DAX I would write the following:

```
Total Sales = SUM(Sales[SalesAmount])
```

This function comprises the following sections:

- Total Sales: This is the name of the measure.
- =: The equals sign indicates the start of the formula. It returns a result when calculated.
- SUM: This DAX function adds up all the numbers in the Sales[SalesAmount] column. We will learn more about functions later.
- (): The parenthesis is used to surround an expression that contains one or more arguments. All functions require at least one argument. An argument passes a value to a function.
- Sales: This is the referenced table.
- [SalesAmount]: This is the referenced column in the Sales table. With this argument, the SUM function knows on which column to aggregate a SUM.

For more information on DAX formulae, please refer to the following site: `https://docs.microsoft.com/en-us/power-bi/transform-model/desktop-quickstart-learn-dax-basics`.

When understanding a DAX formula, it can be helpful to break down each of the elements into common language. For example, you can read this formula as follows:

For the measure named Total Sales, calculate (=) the SUM of values in the [SalesAmount] column in the Sales table.

DAX formulae have been migrated into the logic apps actions catalog. If you can write functions in Excel, you will find that you should be able to do some of the common actions within logic apps natively. If you still need the power of DAX, it is possible to send the data from your logic app to Excel, or to Power BI for further processing, then reuse the returning data to send to your app.

If you have already started to create your own **Power Automate flow apps**, you will have already worked with DAX.

As you can see, enterprise system data manipulation was very much the realm of the programmer. While moving away from proprietary languages such as C/AL was a welcome transition into a more standards-focused language in the form of X++, the move to use C# alongside web pages was in line with other development at the time for **Active Server Page** (**ASP**) development. This led to a complete move away from application code to a focus on pure formula - DAX.

Performing basic mathematical operations

Mathematical operations are very common, and it is reassuring to know that you can calculate these as part of the logic app run. These are commonly used in virtually every flow, function, or logic app I write. To calculate mathematical operations, do this:

1. Initialize your variables (such as a and b). In this exercise, we will set a as 10 and b as 3.

2. Create an output variable to store your answer or create a **Compose** action for the same purpose.

3. Create a **Set variable** action or use the **Compose** action and add the formula to its action field.

What you cannot do is this:

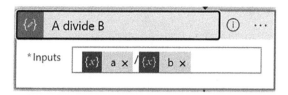

Figure 5.4 – Variable A divided by variable B does not work

This produces 10/3 as a text string.

There are a series of built-in functions for mathematical operations that take the following structure:

```
Function method ( variable 1, variable 2)
```

Let's now discuss some common mathematical functions.

Add

Use the following expression:

```
Add ( variable a , variable b )
```

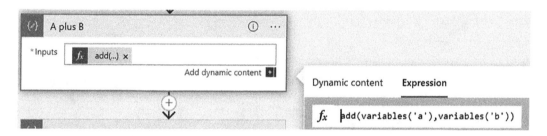

Figure 5.5 – A plus B

This is the expression's syntax:

```
add(variables('a'),variables('b'))
```

Subtract

Use the following expression:

```
Sub ( variable a , variable b )
```

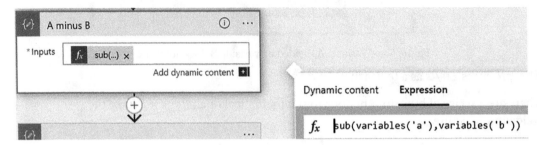

Figure 5.6 – A minus B

Following is the expression's syntax:

```
sub(variables('a'),variables('b'))
```

Multiply

Use the following expression:

```
Mul ( variable a , variable b )
```

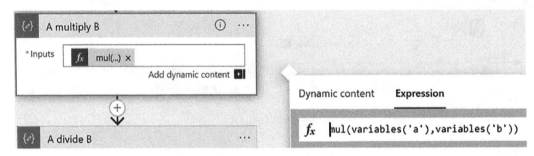

Figure 5.7 – A multiplied by B

This is the expression's syntax:

```
mul(variables('a'),variables('b'))
```

Divide

Use the following expression:

```
Div ( variable a , variable b )
```

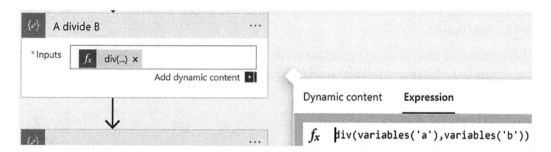

Figure 5.8 – A divided by B

Following is the expression's syntax:

```
div(variables('a'),variables('b'))
```

Remainder (Modulo)

Use the following expression:

```
Mod ( variable a , variable b )
```

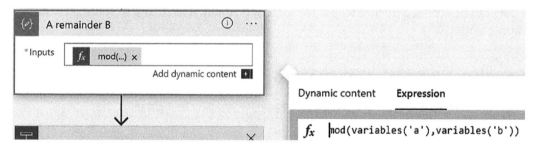

Figure 5.9 – A remainder (modulo) B

This is the expression's syntax:

```
mod(variables('a'),variables('b'))
```

This is only a small selection, but the key point is that you cannot use traditional mathematical symbols within a compose action, rather you need to use the provided functions.

In this section, we have looked at standard mathematical calculations. In the next section, we are going to look at common text string manipulation.

Combining text

There are a few different approaches we can take to concatenate text — some approaches are better than others. Here, I will identify the pain points but also the wins.

Referencing in a compose or set variable action

The easiest way of combining text is to reference them in a compose or set variable action.

Imagine that you have three variables: First Name, Middle Name, and Last Name. You want to combine them to create a **Full Name** field. This would be done as follows.

Set your data into the First Name, Middle Name, and Last Name variables (or compose actions) first. Compose actions are often used for setting data on the fly, and the data can be accessed further within the logic app run by referencing the output of the compose action.

> **Tip**
> Remember to initialize your variables first! This needs to be done at the very start of your logic app. You can only set variables you have brought into existence.

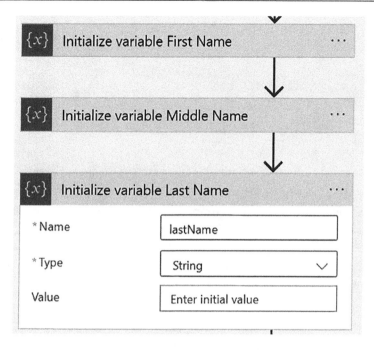

Figure 5.10 – Three initialized variables

In the following screenshot, I am setting a variable with dynamic data:

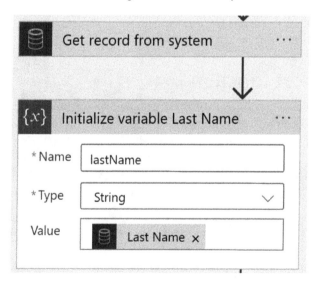

Figure 5.11 – The lastName variable is storing the current dynamic value for Last Name

In this screenshot, I am referencing the previously saved data by using the Output property of the object:

Figure 5.12 – Referencing using the Output from a Compose action

Notice in the preceding screenshot that I have added a space in between each field making up the composited data. Also notice that **compose** actions store the data as a string and implicitly convert your data into a string. Data type conversions between integer and string are not needed when using compose, but if you needed to convert a string to a number you will need to use a function to explicitly perform the conversion.

> **Tip**
>
> It is not necessary to store data using variables when you are working with dynamic data. Usually, you would reference the actual value stored on the **Common Data Service Dataverse**. Set variables are used when manipulating or reformatting data, or to store static data that is unlikely to change during the logic app's run.

Now, let's look at another approach to concatenate text.

Using the concat function

Another simple method to combine all of these into one **Compose** action using the concat(enate) function. This combines the text and allows you to add additional characters (such as when you are building a short date in DD/MM/YYYY format).

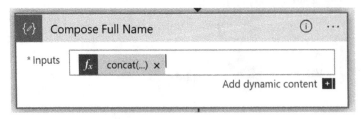

Figure 5.13 – The concat function when correctly saved

> **Tip**
>
> It is very easy to type code in the wrong place, also to look up fields by typing in the **Inputs** field by mistake. The **Dynamic Catalogue** has a search facility to list all parameters, and does so based on the order of the actions nearest to you in the logic app. The search can be used to filter fields to narrow down the search, but it only shows relevant fields from a **Common Data Service** search, usually where the data type matches what you are trying to input.

If the field is not available even once you have clicked the **show all fields** link to reveal all possible fields, you can use **Code view** to add the field manually but remember to use the physical name.

Equally, when working with expressions, remember to use the physical field name, not the logical name as displayed in the graphical interface:

```
concat(body('Get_record_from_system')?['firstname'],body('Get_
record_from_system')?['middlename'],body('Get_record_from_
system')?['lastname'])
```

The following screenshot shows how we use the **Expression** builder for more complex actions:

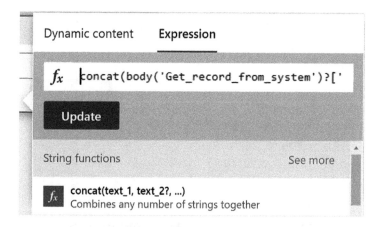

Figure 5.14 – Using the Expression builder

While you can use **Set variable** actions to store your data, I will stick to **Compose** actions for the rest of this chapter. Just remember that the same code will work in either a **Compose** or a **Set variable** action – whichever you prefer to use.

Join actions for arrays

A common problem when working with arrays is how to combine the values into one string. This is often used when working with CSV or XML files, and especially when working with Excel spreadsheets. In the following example, we are converting a one-dimensional array into a string, using commas to make it **Comma Separated Value (CSV)** format so that it can be used in Excel or as part of a system data import:

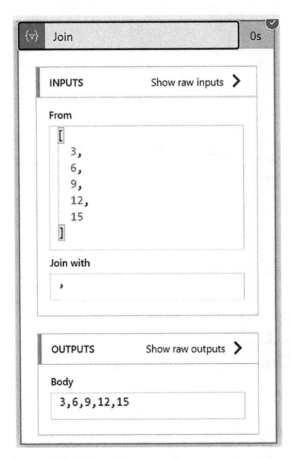

Figure 5.15 – Join action converting an array to a string

Of course, it is always handy to be able to split a string and one of the reasons for this would be to do the reverse of the preceding steps.

String manipulation

By using either index positioning, or by searching for certain characters, we can determine where to split a string to create a substring.

Creating a substring

By using positioning, we can determine where to split a string to create a substring. A substring will return the first section of an array. It uses an index value to mark the starting position and then the number of characters required to return for the output.

If we use our *multiples of 3* array from earlier, with an index position of 0 and a character return count of 3, the first three characters are returned. Notice that I am referencing the 'Join' action we created earlier and examining the body text only:

```
substring(body('Join'),0,3)
```

This screenshot shows the returned output:

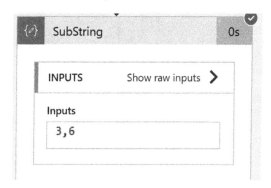

Figure 5.16 – Image showing a substring of the multiples of 3 array

Let's now try counting the length of a string.

Counting the length of a string

By using common DAX functions also available in logic apps, we can quickly determine the length of a string:

```
length(body('Join'))
```

In this screenshot, you can see the input data, as the string is eleven characters long. The **Length** count in the subsequent action confirms this:

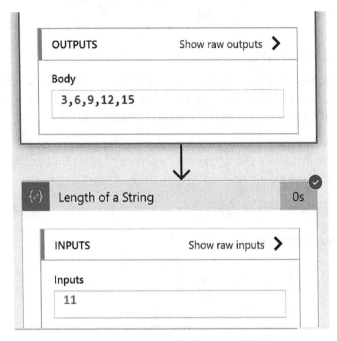

Figure 5.17 – String with the counted value

In this example, the characters of the string have been counted using the Length function, which returns the numeric count of 11. If this were stored in a variable as an integer you will keep the returned data as an integer, but as you are composing, by its very nature the value will be implicitly cast as a string. If you need to represent the data as an integer again either replace the compose with an integer variable or use the Int () function to explicitly recast as a number.

In the next section, we will look at how to determine the pointer position of a character within a string, treating a string as a one-dimensional array starting at position 0.

Index the position of a character in a string

By using common functions, we can determine where a character is located within a string. This can be useful when hunting a long string where a breakpoint symbol such as a comma or pipe is used to identify the next field when parametrizing the string into fields. The `indexOf` expression can be used to locate the first instance of a specific character in a string. We pass the parameters of the variable or object storing the string, then the character we are interested in finding. If this is a symbol, note that I have encapsulated the comma in single quotations. This is because the comma is also a delimiter when writing the expression.

Using the `Join` string from earlier, I am looking for the first comma, which appears at index position 1.

> **Tip**
> An array uses a pointer system, where the storage point for the first character in the string is in fact position 0, not 1. The second character will be in index position 2, and so forth.

We can write the expression as follows:

```
indexOf(body('Join'),',')
```

The output of the action confirms that the first comma is at position 1.

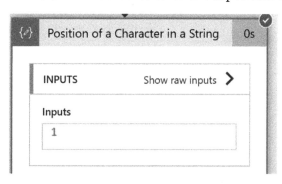

Figure 5.18 – Position of the comma confirmed at index position 1

In this section, you have learned a few basic functions to enable you to navigate through joining, splitting, and counting a string.

Summary

With new expressions and actions being added on a regular basis, this list is by no means exhaustive but is intended to give you a starting point to familiarize yourself with how actions can be used to manipulate data. I did not want this chapter to be a burden, or a difficult one to follow – I wanted you to get an understanding of the concept of expressions and of how expression language is structured. By now, you should be able to perform basic mathematical operations and perform complex manipulations such as combining, splitting, and counting the length of a string.

In the next chapter, we are going to learn how to retrieve and update records to third-party systems and databases using the web-based Common Data Service series of actions.

Section 2: Logic App Design

Section 2 takes a deeper dive into specific commonly used actions and explains how errors can be trapped and used to further refine the logic. We also discuss when it is good practice to split a complex logic app into multiple sequential logic apps and how best to share data between them. This eventually leads you to a point at which you will have a variety of logic apps that you will need to monitor over time to ensure that they are working as intended.

This part of the book comprises the following chapters:

- *Chapter 6, Working with the Common Data Service*
- *Chapter 7, Working with Azure Functions*
- *Chapter 8, Scoping with Try/Catch Error Handling*
- *Chapter 9, Sharing Data with Other Logic Apps and APIs*
- *Chapter 10, Monitoring Logic Apps for Management Reporting*

6
Working with the Common Data Service

Common Data Service (**CDS**) or dataverse is generally accepted and often used across different systems and manufacturers to communicate directly to the system, using dynamic, ever-changing data. It is a suite of connections that allows direct access to your data source, rather than relying on an offline, saved file as was often the case with earlier CSV and XML flat files used to move data from one system to another.

In this chapter, we're going to cover the following main topics:

- Retrieving a record using Get record
- Retrieving a series of records using List records and ForEach
- Updating a record and series of records with ForEach
- Considering how and when to use logical and physical field naming

Technical requirements

As we will again be discussing both OData and JSON messages, I would like to remind you of some of the helpful online validation and formatting tools available:

- **JSONLint** (`https://jsonlint.com`): This is one of many JSON online validators that will not only check your code for errors but also prettify the code, indenting it into a normal JSON structure.

- **JSON Formatter** (`https://jsonformatter.org`): This is also a very useful online site that will format, beautify, but also minify your code, should you need to store it all on one line. The site will also convert your JSON code to CSV, YAML, and XML formats.

- **The JSON Schema tool** (`https://jsonschema.net/home`): This is a great site for generating a JSON schema file, which explains the structure of your JSON message. The schema generated is a full, formal schema so there are quite a lot of elements you don't need, but if you are interested in all possible options that could be stored in the message, this is a good place to check your code.

- **The OData site** (`https://www.odata.org/`): I find this site to be helpful, especially if I need a greater understanding of OData as a general language.

- **OData query reference** (`https://help.nintex.com/en-us/insight/OData/HE_CON_ODATAQueryCheatSheet.htm`): Most of the time, I need to reference OData resources to help me to get my syntax correct when creating OData database queries. The Nintex Hawkeye OData guide is an invaluable reference for the correct spelling of operators and contains plenty of query examples.

The RESTful API

Representational State Transfer (**REST**) is designed to be used when web services connect systems together. As part of this, a conversation takes place between the two systems to determine common speeds to transfer data at, a common language both systems can understand, and status information such as when one system is ready to send or the other is ready to receive. In short, the two systems perform **handshaking** – the process of checking whether a system can receive information, managing the transfer of data using messages, and then closing the connection when the transfer is completed.

At its most basic form, a **GET** or **POST** JSON message to a web service would be a JSON message containing input parameters. The web service has an entry point in the form of a unique web address that the GET request or the POST message would be sent to.

Here is an example GET request with no parameters in the message. The following example can be used to test that the web service is available. If it is available, we should get an error message back from the web service as shown here:

```
Action: GET
URL: https://prod-25.ukwest.logic.azure.com:443/
workflows/35cb47c51c134fe3b395
Body:
{
}
Output: 404 no response.
```

Let's now perform an exercise to test a web service.

Exercise – testing a web service

Follow the given steps to test the web service:

1. In Azure Logic Apps, in your test resource group, add a new object.

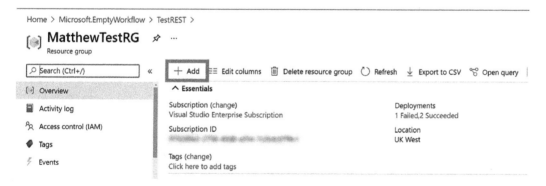

Figure 6.1 – Adding a new object in the resource group

2. In the **Azure Marketplace** catalog, search for `logic apps`.

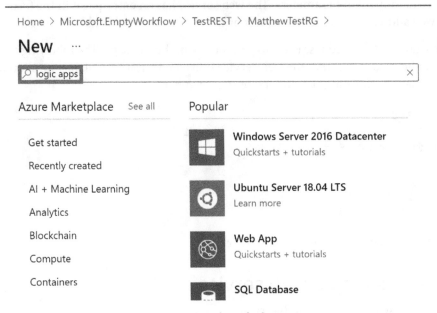

Figure 6.2 – Searching for logic apps

3. From the options presented in the search results, select the traditional **Logic App** option.

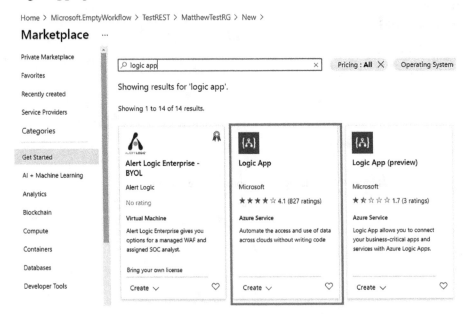

Figure 6.3 – The traditional Logic App option

4. Within the selected tile, press the **Create** button and select **Logic App** from the drop-down list.

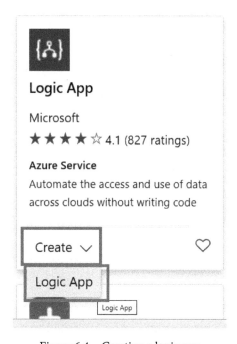

Figure 6.4 – Creating a logic app

5. The logic app creation form opens. Ensure that you have selected your correct subscription and resource group.

Home > MatthewTestRG > New > Marketplace >

Create a logic app   ...

Basics   Tags   Review + create

Create workflows leveraging hundreds of connectors and the visual designer. Learn more ☑

Project details

Select the subscription to manage deployed resources and costs. Use resource groups like folders to organize and manage all your resources.

Subscription *	Visual Studio Enterprise Subscription ⌄
Resource group *	MatthewTestRG ⌄
	Create new

Figure 6.5 – Selecting the subscription and resource group

6. For **Instance details**, select a name. Here I will use `TestREST` and may make several different versions of this logic app. As I have already created `TestREST` for the exercise, which is also stored on this resource group, I am creating a blank logic app called `TestREST_1`.

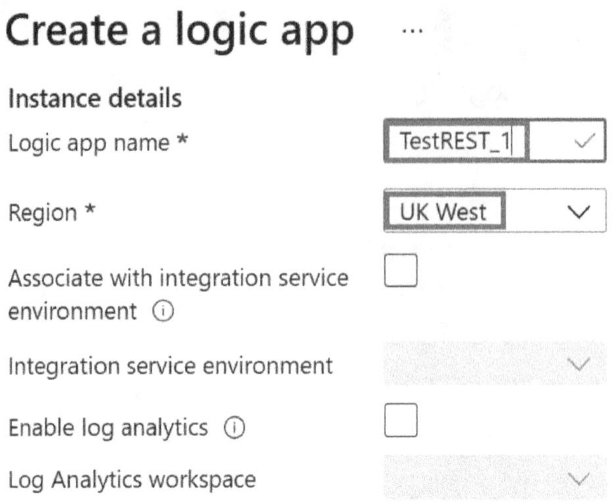

Create a logic app   ...

Instance details

Logic app name * | TestREST_1 | ✓ |

Region * | UK West | ∨ |

Associate with integration service environment ⓘ   ☐

Integration service environment   ∨

Enable log analytics ⓘ   ☐

Log Analytics workspace   ∨

Figure 6.6 – Naming the logic app and deciding which data center to use (Region)

Integration Services is a product offered by Microsoft to perform data translation between JSON, XML, and other formats. It is a paid service, but you could perform the same service within your logic app.

Log Analytics is an auditing tool used when you want to create management pages to track the health, status, and performance of your logic apps. As we don't need to audit this logic app, I have decided not to use this service.

As this is a test logic app, I have decided not to add tags. **Tags** are additional metadata we can add to the object to categorize it and make it easier to search for.

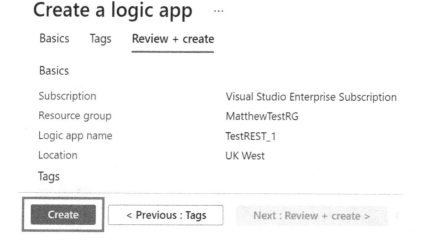

Figure 6.7 – Creating the logic app

Now that the logic app has been created, we can decide to start with a blank canvas or to set one of the common triggers to start our logic app. We are going to need an HTTP request trigger for this exercise.

Logic Apps Designer ⋯

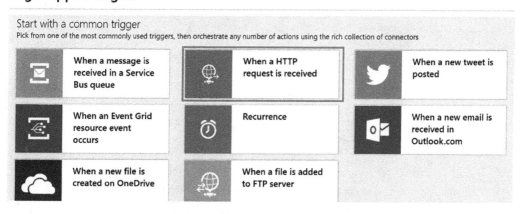

Figure 6.8 – Selecting a common trigger

7. You will now be in the **Logic App Designer** window. Notice that the trigger has been created for you. Note that the URL for this web service will be generated after you have saved the logic app, and that there is a copy button where you can store the URL for this web service.

Also notice that the JSON schema is empty as denoted by the empty curly braces:

```
{ }
```

This means that no input parameters are expected – sending a POST message to this URL will fire the logic app and a status message will be returned. As nothing is set up, I am expecting an error message to indicate that there was nothing to do, but that at least will prove that the web service is functioning.

Save the logic app. At this point, the HTTP POST URL will update with a randomly generated URL, which you can use as an entry point to the web service.

My URL changed to `https://prod-25.ukwest.logic.azure.com:443/workflows/35cb47c51c134fe3b3950b9758593596/triggers/manual/paths/invoke?api-version=2016-10-01&sp=%2Ftriggers%2Fmanual%2Frun&sv=1.0&sig=cUvq70ngszFFzhdLbLA3lrphAg9iY6FfuFd7SrSPmBs.`

8. By clicking on the logic app name in the breadcrumb in the top left of the screen, you will be taken to the overview page for this logic app. Notice that it is **Enabled**. You will be able to track runs by using **Runs history**.

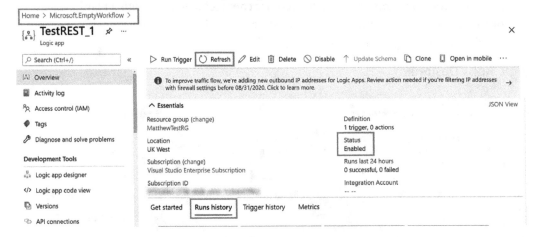

Figure 6.9 – Logic app overview page showing the breadcrumb,
the Refresh button, Status, and Runs history

Remember that at this stage, the logic app is empty. This web service is not designed to do anything yet. Let's test it.

9. Load **Telerik Fiddler** or **Postman** to perform an HTTP POST request (I will be using Postman).

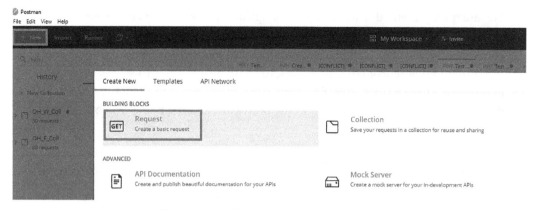

Figure 6.10 – Creating a new HTTP request

10. You will be prompted to name your request and to save the request to a collections folder. If you have not already done so, click + **Create Folder** first. Press the save button to save the message for later use.

Figure 6.11 – Test message named TestTEST_1 in an existing folder with the save button

You are then presented with quite a lot of options, but we only need to use a few. If you are interested in creating complex RESTful messages that are encrypted, contain authentication cookies, or contain more complex authorization mechanics, they can be set here. For basic messages, the bare minimum is to set the direction of travel (GET or POST), the URL where the web service is located, the headers to determine the language being sent in the body text, and the body, which is where we write our message.

Notice that we can also set up **query parameters**. These are a series of key-value pairs (field names containing data) that can be used as input or output parameters.

Finally, notice that the name of our message is **TestTEST_1**. We can change this at any time by editing the title.

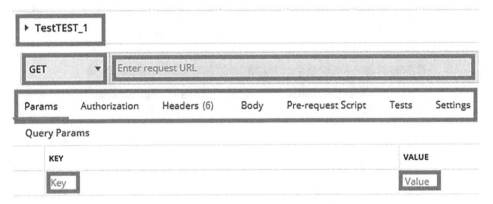

Figure 6.12 – Postman message showing the title, direction, URL, and parameter settings. We are currently on the Params tab

11. In this next step, I have renamed the message. We are looking at the **Body** tab, which by default has an empty message. This means that we will not be sending anything to the web service. Notice that the body language is set to **raw | JSON**. Setting this has the same effect as setting the language type in the header with the following:

```
Content-Type: Application/json
```

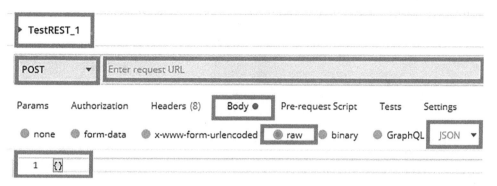

Figure 6.13 – The corrected title, the direction changed to POST, the URL field to add our web service URL, the body tag listing the language as raw JSON, and the empty message

12. Add the URL to the web service in the request URL field and then press **Send**.

Figure 6.14 – Sending the message with the status response

The lower section of the image shows the statistics and return message from the communication when sending to the web service's URL. The **Status** response message with round-trip statistics is shown.

While the response message output is empty, we do indeed get a response from the web service. A 202 message indicates that the web service is up and running and is not waiting for a further reply from our client side.

13. If we switch back to the logic app and refresh the table, we get a **Runs history** item with a unique GUID and even how long the logic app was running for.

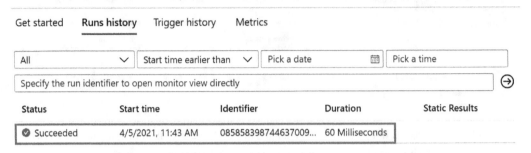

Figure 6.15 – Logic app run history reports the successful message

14. Let's improve the message. Edit the logic app. Add a new step (your first action in this logic app).

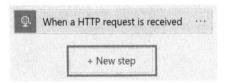

Figure 6.16 – Adding a new action step

15. From the Azure catalog, you should get a recent action of **Request**. This is slightly confusing as **Request** is the name of the suite of actions and what you want to send is a response.

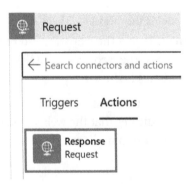

Figure 6.17 – Selecting the Request group reveals the Response action

16. In your new **Response** action, add the following static text to the body:

```
Hello world!
```

17. Save the logic app.

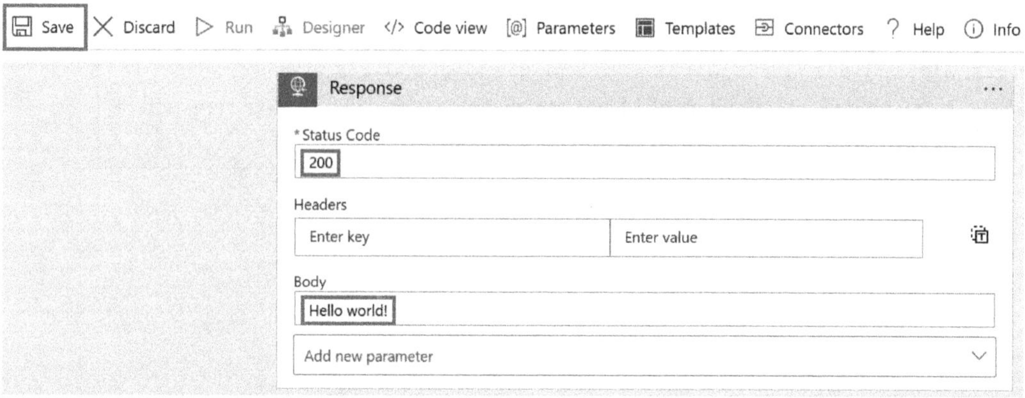

Figure 6.18 – Your first action as a 200 response with a body and the Save button highlighted

Let's look at the JSON code equivalent for the steps.

JSON code

The JSON code looks something like this:

```
"actions": {
        "Response": {
            "runAfter": {},
            "type": "Response",
            "kind": "Http",
            "inputs": {
                "body": "Hello world!",
                "statusCode": 200
            }
        }
    },
```

You will be prompted with an Azure status message to inform you that the logic app has been saved successfully.

ⓘ Save logic app completed   11:58 AM ✕
Logic app: TestREST_1 was saved successfully

Figure 6.19 – Logic app has been saved

The Azure status message appears briefly at the top right of the screen to notify you of the save.

> **Tip**
> If any actions are not interlinked and parameters are missing, the logic app will not save until these omissions have been rectified.

Rerun the Postman message. You will now get a return message.

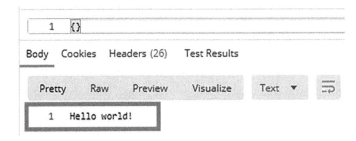

Figure 6.20 – Postman call with the return message output

Excellent! To quote Dr. Frankenstein – "It's alive!"

In this next section, we're going to make the data more complex by passing `Key:Value` JSON pairs as our input and output data.

Extension task

Please follow the given steps to perform the extension task:

1. Amend the JSON Postman message to list a `Key:Value` parameter we can use within the web service. Amend the message to the following code:

    ```
    {"Firstname":"Matthew"}
    ```

2. Edit the logic app. In **Trigger**, use the **Use sample payload to generate schema** link and paste the body from your previous message into the generator.

    Enter or paste a sample JSON payload.

    ```
    {"Firstname":"Matthew"}
    ```

Figure 6.21 – Generator containing the JSON payload from your message body

3. Press **Done**.

The trigger will be amended to include an object that contains a parameter called `Firstname`, which will hold data of the `string` type:

```
{
    "type": "object",
    "properties": {
        "Firstname": {
            "type": "string"
        }
    }
}
```

4. In the **Response** action's **Body** field, amend the message to read `Hello <Body>!`, where `Body` is the body of the trigger as found in the **Dynamic content** catalog.

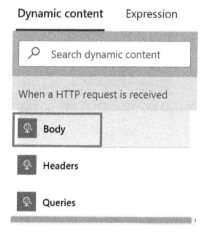

Figure 6.22 – Dynamic catalog listing Body from the trigger

Is this correct? No. This will return the entirety of the data portion of the message, so if we run this, we will get the following:

```
Hello {"Firstname":"Matthew"}!
```

You will, however, notice that because we have provided a schema for the trigger, the message can be parsed and the **Firstname** parameter is available from the dynamic catalog as well.

Here is the amended **Response** action with the new, correct dynamic parameter:

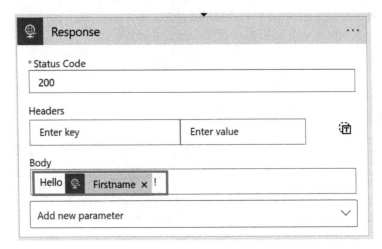

Figure 6.23 – Response action set to return a dynamic response

5. Finally, upon resending the message in Postman, you get a successful 200 message with the correct return message:

```
Hello Matthew!
```

Notice the time breakdown lists how long each stage of the round-trip took.

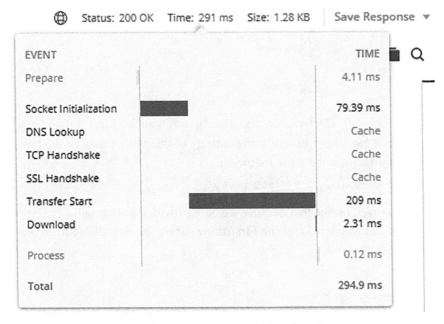

Figure 6.24 – Message round-trip timings from Postman

In this section, you have been able to use Postman to send a message to a logic app that has processed the data you have provided, calculated certain values, and returned an output all within the space of 294.9 milliseconds!

Let's extend our understanding of actions within a logic app to include calls to database application systems such as Salesforce or Dynamics 365.

Retrieving a record with CDS

CDS is an application-level suite of actions designed to obtain a record or list of records from an entity. It can also be used to create or update records within the entity.

As CDS operates as a web service, not a direct link to the underlying database used by the web system, any validation that is present at the application level will be applied to the CDS action. Data requests will be screened in much the same way as searching for a particular record within the CRM environment. For this reason, you need to decide whether it is the appropriate choice for you to use.

Pros and cons

There are many reasons to see CDS (later referenced as the Microsoft Dataverse) as superior to Dynamics 365 connections, which have now been deprecated. Reasons for this include the following:

- Microsoft recommends CDS.
- Dynamics 365, Salesforce, and other application action sets are being replaced with CDS actions.
- CDS is easier to set up and manipulate than deprecated actions.
- Older Dynamics 365 actions operate on a timer, whereas CDS actions trigger instantly on a create, update, or delete action.
- CDS triggers can be filtered to a specific field or set of fields being updated; only if the field is in scope will the trigger fire.

However, the following are a few cons of CDS:

- CDS actions are not direct writes to the database.
- Creating a record via CDS means that the data is subject to scrutiny on the application level in much the same way as completing a form on the CRM.
- CDS cannot be used effectively for data cleansing where validation would be most easily triaged by an update query on the underlying database.

Given this, let's look at one of the most used CDS actions – the Get record action – which finds one specific record by ID and returns the full entity.

Retrieving a record using the Get record action

We are going to use our CRM alongside our previously built logic app to return details from a contact record. I have already looked up a test contact record from the CRM. We are going to continue with the earlier exercise by adding data from our CRM.

Exercise

Follow these steps to retrieve a record using the Get record action:

1. On your CRM, navigate to your test account and record the contact ID (GUID).

2. Update your Postman call, replacing the name of the field with `ContactID` and the data with your GUID, as follows:

```
{"ContactID":"0d4685c5-ac04-eb11-a813-000d3a86ba0b"}
```

3. In your logic app, on the trigger, press **Use sample payload to generate schema** and paste your new message into the generator.

   Notice that only the name of the field has changed:

```
{
    "type": "object",
    "properties": {
        "ContactID": {
            "type": "string"
        }
    }
}
```

4. Between the trigger and the existing **Response** action, press the plus button to add a new action at this point.

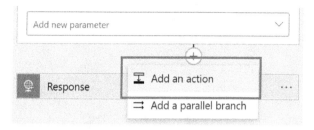

Figure 6.25 – Adding a new action

> **Tip**
>
> Adding a parallel branch will do just that – a separate action branch will be added at this point. For this exercise, we are going to be running the logic app in series, so we need to use **Add an action**.

5. From the dynamic catalog, select the **Common Data Service** suite of actions. If this is not present, use the **Search connectors and actions** field to look for **Get record**.

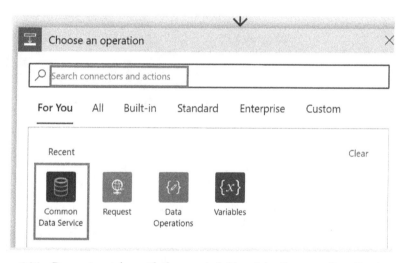

Figure 6.26 – Dynamic catalog with the search field and the Common Data Service suite

6. From the suite, select **Get record**. Populate the action as follows:

A. **Environment**: Select your own environment. I will use my **Development** environment.

B. **Entity Name: Contact** (or alternative).

C. **Item identifier**: Select **ContactID** from the **Trigger** section of the dynamic catalog.

Your action should look something like this:

Figure 6.27 – Get record action listing the Environment, Entity Name, and Item identifier fields

Here is the action in code view:

```
"Get_record": {
              "inputs": {
                  "host": {
                      "connection": {
                          "name": "@
parameters('$connections')['commondataservice']
['connectionId']"
                      }
                  },
                  "method": "get",
                  "path": "/v2/datasets/@{encodeURI
Component(encodeURIComponent('b3ae00f4c2054abc123ce4
56789d01.crm11'))}/tables/@{encodeURIComponent(encodeURI
Component('contacts'))}/items/@{encodeURIComponent
(encodeURIComponent(triggerBody()?['ContactID']))}"
              },
              "runAfter": {},
              "type": "ApiConnection"
          },
```

Now that you have included the Get record action, your choice of parameters will be more extensive as you can now include the fields from your contact.

7. In the **Response** action, amend the body as follows:

A. Remove the **Firstname** dynamic parameter as this is no longer in use.

B. Add **Title**, **First Name**, and **Last Name** from the dynamic catalog.

Your amended action should look like this (ensure to correctly space the sentence):

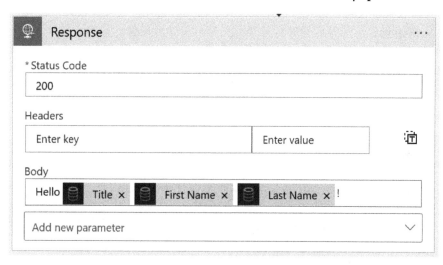

Figure 6.28 – Amended action with CDS logical names

Let's now look at the JSON code equivalent for the steps.

JSON code

Here is the Response action as JSON code, as available in code view:

```
"Response": {
            "runAfter": {
                "Get_record": [
                    "Succeeded"
                ]
            },
            "type": "Response",
            "kind": "Http",
            "inputs": {
                "body": "Hello @{body('Get_
record')?['titleid_value']} @{body('Get_
record')?['firstname']} @{body('Get_record')?['lastname']}!",
                "statusCode": 200
            }
        }
    },
```

Save your logic app and return to the **Overview** page.

Rerun your Postman call with the new message.

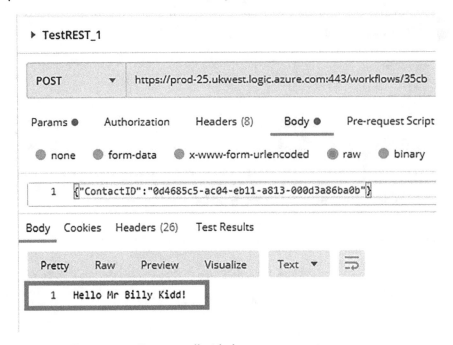

Figure 6.29 – Postman call with the new return output message

Now you're getting the hang of it. You've refined the earlier logic app to perform a call to your CRM, retrieve a specific record, and from this, return an output, in this case, the full name of your customer.

Let's work on this some more to retrieve plural records by using the similar List records action.

Retrieving a series of records using List records and ForEach

Get record has one limitation – you need to already know the record you are interested in and need to use its GUID (its primary key identifier) to call the record in full. If we want to obtain a series of records that meet given criteria, we use **List records**.

Exercise

We are going to amend the logic app to return a series of names and then send these back in one message to Postman in the following steps:

1. Remove the **Get record** action and the dynamic parameters from the **Response** action's body.

> **Tip**
>
> To remove an action, or to rename it, click the more button (three dots) on the right of the action's title, and from the list of settings, select **Delete**.

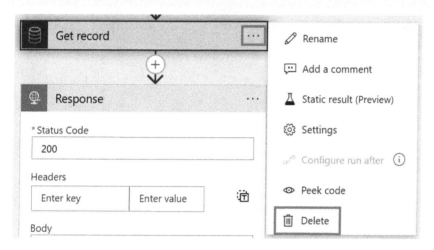

Figure 6.30 – The more and Delete buttons

2. In place of **Get record**, add **List records** from the **Common Data Service** suite using the same method as **Get record** earlier.

3. Set the action with the following parameters:

    A. **Environment**: Select your own environment. I will use my **Development** environment.

    B. **Entity Name: Contact** (or alternative).

4. Click the **Add new parameter** dropdown and select **Filter query**. This allows you to create an OData query to determine the values you want.

> **Tip**
> Note that CDS provides logical names, not physical names. In code view, however, you will see the physical names. OData also uses physical names.

5. For our OData query, I want to list all the people with the surname `Smith`. This would be written as follows:

```
lastname eq 'Smith'
```

6. I am only interested in the top five records, so I have also filled in the **Top Count** parameter.

Figure 6.31 – List records with a filter query and a top count

As you are looking for records based on your search criteria, let's amend the JSON request message to work with this section of the logic app.

7. In Postman, amend the message to the following:

```
{
    "lastName":"Smith",
    "topCount":5
}
```

8. In the logic app, generate a new schema as demonstrated earlier. Your schema will now change to the following:

```
{
    "type": "object",
    "properties": {
        "lastName": {
            "type": "string"
        },
        "topCount": {
            "type": "integer"
        }
    }
}
```

9. Save your logic app.

The physical fields from your input message can now be used in your OData query.

In your **List records** action, amend **Filter Query** and **Top Count** to use the input fields from the trigger. Please ensure that the `lastname` parameter from our trigger, which contains our input data, is encapsulated with single quotes to force the OData query to treat this data as a string. (The OData query will not know that this is a string.)

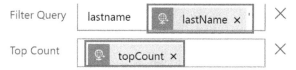

Figure 6.32 – List records action using the new input fields. Note the single quotes

We are expecting more than one record to be returned, so we need to loop through the data and obtain all responses.

10. Below the **List records** action, add a new action. In the **Control** suite of actions, select **For each**, or search for this in the search field.

What will it loop through? We want to look through all the values of the List records action, so in the **Select an output from the previous steps** field, select **value** from the dynamic catalog.

11. Within the **For each** section, select **Add an action**. We are going to collate all the found names and return this to Postman as a string, so from the **Variables** section of the dynamic catalog, select **Append to string variable**.

12. Your **For each** block should look like this:

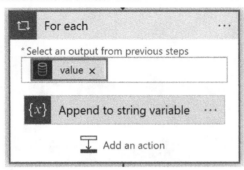

Figure 6.33 – For each section linked to the List records action

So now, for every record found that meets the criteria, the data you have asked for will be added as a new component to your array.

JSON code

Here is the JSON code for your **For each** action:

```
"For_each": {
            "foreach": "@body('List_records')?['value']",
            "actions": {
                "Append_to_string_variable": {
                    "runAfter": {},
                    "type": "AppendToStringVariable",
                    "inputs": {
                        "name": "names",
                        "value": "Hello @{items('For_
each')?['firstname']} @{items('For_each')?['lastname']}!"
                    }
                }
            },
            "runAfter": {
                "List_records": [
                    "Succeeded"
                ]
            },
            "type": "Foreach"
        },
```

Before we can proceed, we need to create a variable to store our names. As the For each action loops through the different names, we would like to add our newly found names to this list. For this, we need to initialize a variable to store this data:

1. Go back to your trigger. Underneath the trigger, select **Add an action**, and from the variables suite, select **Initialize variable**. Set the variable to the following:

    A. **Name**: names.

    B. **Type**: string.

    C. **Value**: Leave empty.

2. Go back to your **For each** section. In the **Append to string variable** action, select the name as **names** from the list.

    Set **Value** to the following:

    ```
    Hello <First Name> <Last Name>!,
    ```

    The completed action should look like this:

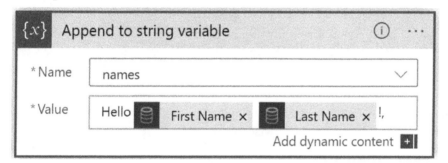

Figure 6.34 – The names variable with values from the List records action

3. Finally, in the **Response** action, remove the existing data in the body and replace it with the **names** variable.

    By doing this, you will get a comma-separated list of the found names.

In Postman, resend the message. Here is my return output:

Figure 6.35 – Postman return output

> **Tip**
> Notice that the final message has a comma at the end. As an extension activity, try to remove this by removing the final character of the data stored in **names**.

In this exercise, you have created a CSV file of a list of names from your CRM system that meets given criteria.

One of the greatest benefits of using a **ForEach** loop is to update data in a second system where there is a match. I often use this technique to migrate data from a test system into a production system or from two otherwise incompatible systems. Let's look at how we can do this.

Updating a record and series of records with ForEach

The preceding exercise can be reversed – you can easily update records found in one system that already exist in another. In my example, I have a *sandbox* environment and a *development* environment. Both contain similar sets of data and are created from the same data image (so the GUIDs will match), but the data in the sandbox is old and needs to be refreshed with data from the development environment. We can extend our ForEach section to update the records.

Exercise – updating a record in an existing environment

For this exercise, we will update Dave and Hayley (who are both doctors) to have the "Dr." title.

In my CRM system, I first obtain from Power Automate, or from checking the **Contact Types** lookup, the GUID for the **Dr** record. As my CRM is using lookups to other sub-entities as opposed to optionset values, GUIDs are used to identify the record in question:

1. I first navigate to the **Person Contact Title** record for the **Dr** title.

Figure 6.36 – The Dr record in my CRM

2. In the address URL for this record, I notice that the contact title ID is displayed:

    ```
    ....contacttitle&id=c98f7542-2d74-ea11-a813-000d3a86b618
    ```

    I record the GUID for future reference:

    ```
    c98f7542-2d74-ea11-a813-000d3a86b618
    ```

3. In the logic app, near the top, I create a **Compose** action to store this GUID. It looks something like this:

Figure 6.37 – Compose action storing the title GUID

> **Tip**
>
> Depending on the design of your CRM's architecture, you may be presented with a **Title Value** option within the **Update a record** action, which contains the selection as text. If this is present, use this. If this is not present, you will need to reference the lookup value by its GUID as previously.

4.   Here is the completed action:

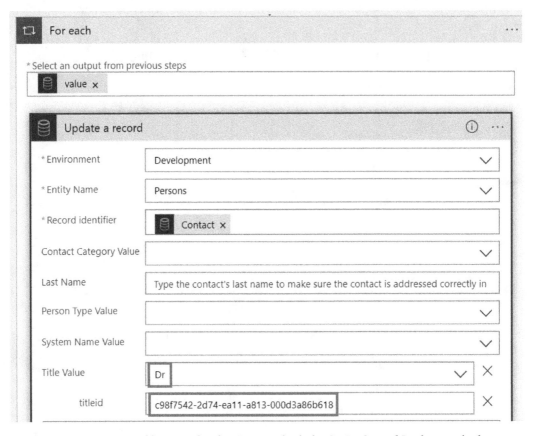

Figure 6.38 – Record being updated to Dr using both the OptionSet and Lookup methods

As you can see, we are setting every person found with the title of **Dr** – I do hope they've earned it!

JSON code

This is the JSON code for the For each action, in code view:

```json
"For_each": {
                "foreach": "@body('List_records')?['value']",
                "actions": {
                    "Update_a_record": {
                        "runAfter": {},
                        "type": "ApiConnection",
                        "inputs": {
                            "body": {
                                "title": 143570005,
                                "titleid": "c98f7542-2d74-ea11-
a813-000d3a86b618"
                            },
                            "host": {
                                "connection": {
                                    "name": "@
parameters('$connections')['commondataservice']
['connectionId']"
                                }
                            },
                            "method": "patch",
                            "path": "/v2/datasets/@{encodeURI
Component(encodeURIComponent('b3ae00f4c2054abc123ce456789d01.
crm11'))}/tables/@{encodeURIComponent(encodeURIComponent
('contacts'))}/items/@{encodeURIComponent(encodeURIComponent
(items('For_each')?['contactid']))}"
                        }
                    }
                },
                "runAfter": {
                    "List_records": [
                        "Succeeded"
                    ]
                },
                "type": "Foreach"
            },
```

After running the logic app from a Postman call, both contacts are updated in the CRM.

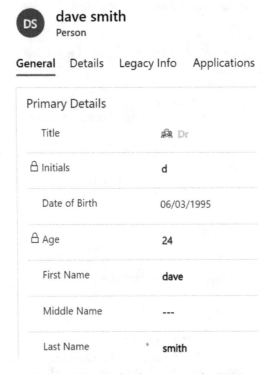

Figure 6.39 – Updated contact in the CRM

As you can see in the preceding example, **dave smith** is now **Dr dave smith**!

We've referenced fields slightly differently within the logic app, as I am sure you will have noticed. In design mode, you see logical names; however, if you hover over the field with your mouse, or go into code view, you will see the physical name for the field. In the next section, we will look at the differences in how we can access fields.

How and when to use logical and physical field naming

In summary, a data field can be referenced in one of three ways:

- On the CRM itself, every data field has a label. The label contains label data and the label object on the form has a label object name. This, however, has no bearing on the data field it is associated with.

- Labels sit next to data fields. These have a logical name and only the logical name is visible from the GUID. CDS will also reference the logical name. Searches in the dynamic catalog will uncover fields by their logical name.

- OData queries and references to parameters or fields in Logic Apps code view refer to the physical name of the field. SQL queries likewise operate at this lower level when addressing the database. The physical name of the CDS field is the physical name within the database.

As a rule of thumb, we should use logical names where the Dynamics 365 field is correctly indexed. If it is a custom field, it might not exist in the catalog as a field we can choose. If you are referencing an action outside of a ForEach loop, the field may again not be accessible. However, if using code view, you have a surefire way of ensuring that you are accessing the correct field.

Summary

In this chapter, we have looked at the use of RESTful data by creating a web service. This was extended to dealing with dynamic data from the input message. We then adapted our exercise to get a known record, then to list records by criteria and return the findings as an output message to Postman.

We then extended this further by updating a series of records with given criteria specified in the Postman message.

Finally, we looked at where we use logical, in contrast to physical, field naming to access our fields. We learned that CDS operates at the application level, and that the logic app dynamic catalog is also logical in its structure, but code view and OData queries use the physical field name.

This chapter has tested not only your JSON but also your abilities with logic and how to cycle through records, the scoping of data, and how to best query records using OData, as well as direct access using a Get records action and a given GUID.

In our next chapter, we are going to uncover Azure functions, as some more complex manipulation may require a C# app. The next chapter will look at how you can use your function within a logic app.

7
Working with Azure Functions

While logic apps allow you to perform most common actions, some more complex manipulation may require a C# app. This chapter looks at how you can use your function within a logic app.

In this chapter you will learn how to do the following:

- Send data to an Azure Function from a logic app to perform advanced functions.
- Retrieve data from an Azure Function to use the data within the remainder of the logic app.

The chapter will cover the following main topics:

- Understanding an Azure Function
- Sending data to an Azure Function from a logic app
- Retrieving data from an Azure Function

Technical requirements

The following are the technical requirements for this chapter:

- JSONLint
- JSON Formatter
- The JSON Schema tool
- The OData site
- An OData query reference
- Knowledge of XML and SQL queries is also required

Understanding an Azure function

An Azure function is a piece of code or application that is stored within your Azure account as an object. It is a **Platform-as-a-Service (PaaS)** offering and provides on-demand execution capabilities. Further details can be found at `https://azure.microsoft.com/en-gb/pricing/details/functions/`.

The object is published to a **resource group**. This object can be accessed by a logic app, which can pass data into the function as input parameters and work on the output that's returned.

Functions can be written in a variety of ways but commonly, they are written as *C#* console apps for use in data formatting or calculations, which cannot easily be done within a logic app alone.

Therefore, if you want to take advantage of the entire .NET Framework's suite of code, which is more extensive than the logic app, or you want to customize your app so that it's tailored to your needs and you can do so easier than within a C# app, you can create and test the app offline. Then, when you are ready, you can publish the app as an **Azure Function** to your resource group.

Mind your language

Azure functions are written within a code editor, such as *Netbeans, Eclipse,* or *Visual Studio.* The most common way to do this today is to use *Visual Studio Code* (the version specifically designed for use with Azure). The most common language that's used to create apps is C#, which is a high-level language that uses Microsoft's .NET Framework of code. Java is also popular and is quite low-level and strict, meaning that you only write the code you need to use and as such, your application is often quite small and specific in its design. PowerShell scripts can also be used. Interestingly, Python scripts can also be used as a code sequence. For further information, you can refer to the documentation of *C#, Java, JavaScript, PowerShell,* or *Python.*

Serverless code

Azure functions exist as objects and simply work. In earlier systems, you had to build a web application server (such as **Internet Information Services** (**IIS**) or Apache) to host your app, then communicate with it on the **localhost** socket. In earlier days, with Azure, you had to build a **virtual machine** (**VM**) manually or with **Docker** to spin up an Apache server and then install your code on that server, then expose your VM's firewall to allow the Azure cloud to access the VM before you could use your app. Now, it just works.

Benefits of working with an Azure function

There are multiple scenarios where you might wish to consider enhancing your logic app by using an Azure function:

- You can interface your web app with other resources, including a logic app, by using an **HTTP Trigger** function. This will allow you to communicate with your app.

- Files can be uploaded, changed, or have metadata added to them.

- A series of existing functions can be combined to form a sequence of functions known as a **serverless workflow**. This can be useful if you have atomic, specific functions and want to meet the requirements of a business process using existing code.

- If you are creating or updating records in an Azure-hosted database, you may want a listener to determine when a change has occurred, which will allow you to start a series of secondary tasks or alert the user of a change. In the logic app, I often send out email alerts or a flow card via *Teams* to the originator, to inform them if their data is missing an important field and that the logic app was unable to process it due to this missing or incorrect data.

- As with any code, you can assign an Azure function so that it runs against a schedule, ensuring that events such as data cleanup or bulk updating status flags can occur during non-working hours.

- You might decide to create a series of messages from a gateway and store these for use by other logic apps or apps. By building a message queueing system using Azure *Queue Storage*, *Service Bus*, or *Event Hubs*, we can start other logic apps based on certain audited actions.

- You may be linking to bots or **Internet of Things (IoT)** internet-enabled hardware devices and need a mechanism to process the data that's been collected. For example, Alexa is a hardware display and speaker/microphone with a "personality." All the questions that are asked to it by the user are converted from speech into text. Then, the text is processed as a question or instruction. The catalog of events Alexa can respond to must be pre-programmed, but this is done as part of the functions that drive Alexa.

- We can also use functions or **SignalR** to respond directly to certain data being presented in real time.

Now, let's see how to create an Azure function.

Exercise – how to create an Azure function

In this exercise, you will be using the **Visual Studio Code** application to create a *C#* class function that responds to HTTP requests. Then, we will test the code locally and deploy it as an Azure Function.

Requirements

You will need to install the following software:

- An Azure account, as detailed in *Chapter 1*, *Getting Started with Azure Logic Apps*.

- **Azure Functions Core Tools**. This can be found here: `https://docs.microsoft.com/en-us/azure/azure-functions/functions-run-local#install-the-azure-functions-core-tools`.

- The Visual Studio Code application. This can be installed from here: `https://code.visualstudio.com/`.

I am making the presumption here that you have a local administrator account on your machine, and that you also have standard default firewall settings that will not block access to your Azure space. Other prerequisites are available via the preceding links.

Once you have installed Visual Studio Code, you will also need to add the
following extensions:

- The *C#* extension for Visual Studio Code. This can be obtained from the *extensions*
  gallery, or from here: `https://marketplace.visualstudio.com/`
  `items?itemName=ms-dotnettools.csharp`.

- The Azure Functions extension for Visual Studio Code. This can be obtained from
  the *Extensions* gallery, or from here: `https://marketplace.visualstudio.`
  `com/items?itemName=ms-azuretools.vscode-azurefunctions`.

Here is the list of installed extensions. Once installed, you should see the two new
extensions here:

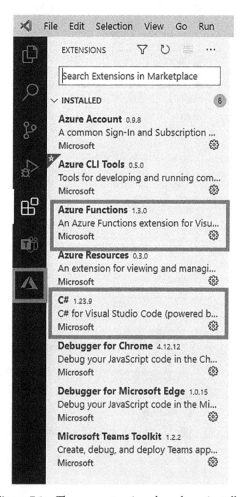

Figure 7.1 – The new extensions have been installed

Notice that the Azure logo appears on the left blade, confirming that the extension has been installed.

Caveats

There are no caveats for this installation. Please use the installation wizards with their default settings.

Creating your Azure Functions project

So, where to begin? As a reminder, an Azure function is simply a standard dynamic-link library or **EXE** file function, typically written in *C#* as part of a larger application. It just so happens to be hosted in the Azure cloud, which makes it easy to access from your Azure tenant.

> **Note**
>
> If you have Visual Studio Code still open after installing the preceding extensions, please exit it formally to update Visual Studio Code's settings; otherwise, the extensions will not be live.

Follow these steps to set up your Azure functions project:

1. Open Visual Studio Code.
2. On the **Activity** blade (the last section of the screen), select the **Azure** icon.
3. From the Azure **Functions** page, go to the **Functions** area and click on **Create New Project**. This can be done by selecting the action or the button:

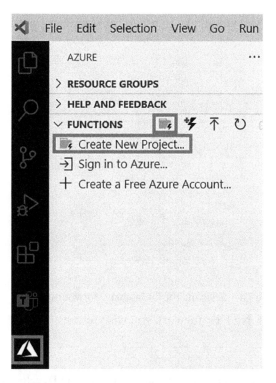

Figure 7.2 – Azure Functions blade listing the two buttons to create a new project

You will now be presented with a pop-up window, asking you where you would like to store your new project:

> **Tip**
> Create the folder first, within your local drive's structure.

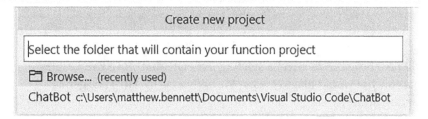

Figure 7.3 – Selecting where to create your new project

4. Select the language you would like to use to develop your function. We will be using **C#**:

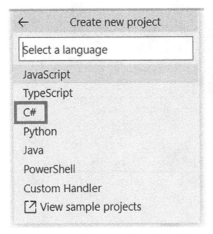

Figure 7.4 – Selecting the C# language for your function

5. Select the version of .NET Framework you wish to use:

> **Note**
>
> You need to have installed the appropriate .NET **Software Development Kit (SDK)** for it to be available as an option for Visual Studio Code.

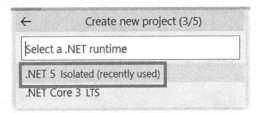

Figure 7.5 – Selecting the appropriate SDK to use

6. You will now be asked to select a starting template that closely resembles the function you would like to create. We will be using **HttpTrigger** as our starting project:

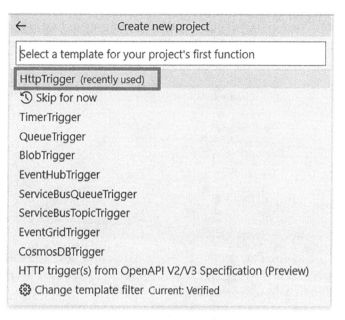

Figure 7.6 – Selecting HttpTrigger as your startup project

7. Provide a name for your project. I will call mine `HttpFunctionMJB`:

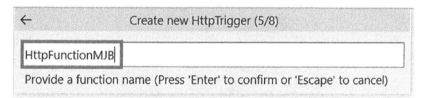

Figure 7.7 – Adding a project name

8. Provide a namespace for your function to operate within. A namespace is the overarching "catch-all" name for all the methods, parameters, and functions you wish to interact with each other. I will name my namespace `My.MJBFunctions`:

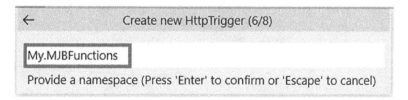

Figure 7.8 – Naming the namespace

9. We can restrict access to the function by determining an authorization level. Here, we will allow anyone with access to the URL to communicate with the app by setting this to **Anonymous** access:

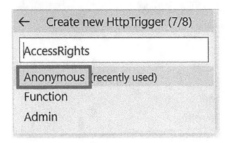

Figure 7.9 – Setting authorization for Anonymous access

Finally, you can choose to open the project in a new window or add it to your Visual Studio Code workspace. This is a personal preference, but I like to have everything in one place, so I have chosen to **Add to workspace**.

Visual Studio Code takes a moment to prepare the project, creating templated code for you to get started.

On the left of the workspace, you will notice that the **Functions** section of the **Azure** blade now contains your new, local project:

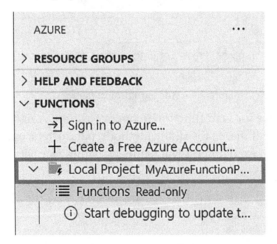

Figure 7.10 – Azure blade with a new local project

In the status bar at the bottom left of your screen, you will see that you are working on your new project:

Figure 7.11 – Visual Studio Code status bar

In the main section of the workspace, you will see that the default *C#* file has been created for you. This contains your namespace and main function:

```csharp
using System.Collections.Generic;
using System.Net;
using Microsoft.Azure.Functions.Worker;
using Microsoft.Azure.Functions.Worker.Http;
using Microsoft.Extensions.Logging;

namespace My.MJBFunctions
{
    public static class HttpFunctionMJB
    {
        [Function("HttpFunctionMJB")]
        public static HttpResponseData Run([HttpTrigger
(AuthorizationLevel.Anonymous, "get", "post")]
HttpRequestData req,
            FunctionContext executionContext)
        {
            var logger = executionContext.GetLogger
("HttpFunctionMJB");
            logger.LogInformation("C# HTTP trigger function
processed a request.");

            var response = req.CreateResponse(HttpStatusCode.
OK);
            response.Headers.Add("Content-Type", "text/
plain; charset=utf-8");

            response.
WriteString("Welcome to Azure Functions!");

            return response;
        }
    }
}
```

The function does very little now but should at least provide a response in the terminal. To test this, press *F5* on your keyboard to start the Function App project.

Tip

If you are trying to run Visual Studio Code from behind an application firewall, remember that the application will try to install and restore any dependencies needed by the application. This project requires access to the NuGet expansions library. You will need to ensure that your administrator has allowed you to access this site. If you are a home user or working from a public area, you will not face this restriction.

We are now at a point where the function should work functionally but is reliant on external, additional plugins that haven't been installed yet. To resolve this, we are going to use the NuGet catalog to add external references and plugins that are provided as part of the Microsoft community.

Exploring the issues of NuGet

Out of the box, your project will compile with errors as it was unable to download the **NuGet** extensions for your project. You need to do two things to correct this:

1. Sign up to NuGet.org and give your consent for NuGet to use your Microsoft account.

2. From the **Output** pane, right-click and select **Command Palette**. From the list of actions, select **.NET: Restore Project**. This will download any required libraries and extensions needed for this project from NuGet:

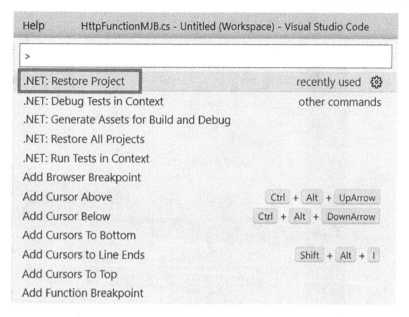

Figure 7.12 – .NET: Restore Project is available from the Command Palette

Now that we have an error-free project, we can build on it. Pressing the *F5* function key will start the build process. Looking at the terminal window, the build will take up to a minute to complete and will end with an entry point URL you can use to test the app:

```
Azure Functions Core Tools
Core Tools Version:      3.0.3388 Commit hash: fb42a4e0b7fdc85fbd0bcfc8d743ff7d509122ae
Function Runtime Version: 3.0.15371.0

[2021-04-07T15:03:07.855Z] Found C:\Users\matthew.bennett\Documents\Visual Studio Code\MyAzureFunctionProject\MyAzureFunctionProj
ect.csproj. Using for user secrets file configuration.

Functions:

        HttpFunctionMJB: [GET,POST] http://localhost:7071/api/HttpFunctionMJB

For detailed output, run func with --verbose flag.
[2021-04-07T15:03:22.119Z] Host lock lease acquired by instance ID '000000000000000000000000EF1DFA21'.
```

Figure 7.13 – Final section of the build showing the URL to test your app

3. Go back to the **Azure** blade. You will notice that your function is now available in the local **Functions** section:

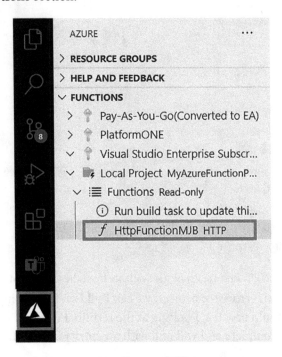

Figure 7.14 – HttpFunctionMJB is now active

> **Tip**
>
> If your function is not in the **Functions** list, click on **Run build task to update this list** to refresh it.

4. To test the function, right-click on the function and select **Execute Function Now**.

5. We need to send it an input message. Let's send the following JSON message:

```
{ "name": "Matthew" }
```

A pop-up window will appear where you can send your input message:

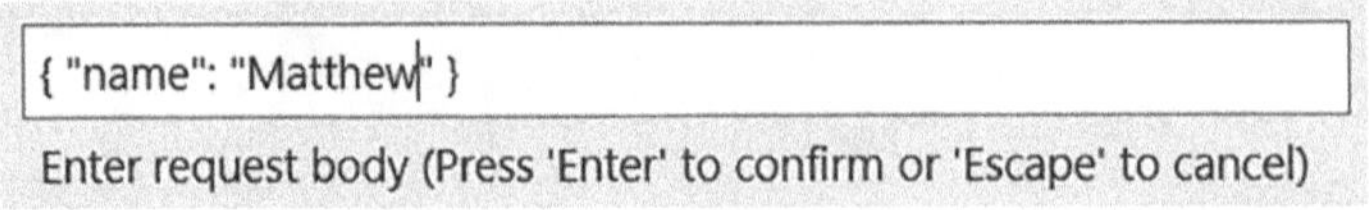

{ "name": "Matthew" }

Enter request body (Press 'Enter' to confirm or 'Escape' to cancel)

Figure 7.15 – An input field appears

However, my attempt did not work initially. The reason for this is that the default option is to run your project in the Azure cloud, and the project hasn't been set up to work with the cloud yet. We need to test it locally first.

Since you have installed Azure Functions Core Tools, effectively, your machine is a local web server and can test code to be sent to Azure. To fix this, we need to ask Visual Studio Code to run the project offline.

6. From the leftmost blade, select the **Run** button to bring up the **Run** pane. From the **RUN AND DEBUG** drop-down list, change the option to **Attach to .NET Functions**. This will run your code locally:

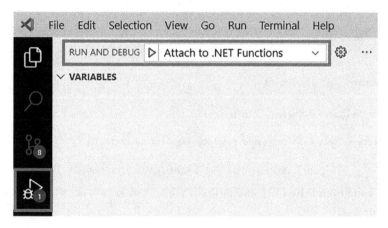

Figure 7.16 – Setting the project to run locally

7. Run the project and as we did previously, pass the JSON message. You will get the following output in the message window:

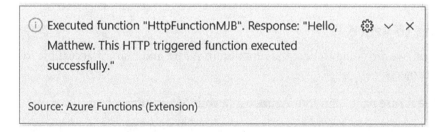

Figure 7.17 – Message window containing your response

Alternatively, you can test this in *Postman*. Set up a POST call to the localhost URL with the body set to **raw:JSON** and containing your message, as we did previously in this exercise:

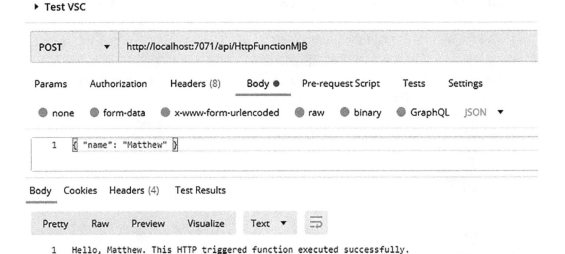

Figure 7.18 – Postman POST message and response

8. Finally, if you amend the URL and suffix it with `"name"="Matthew"`, you will get the same message.

And there we have it! You have created a function, added NuGet extensions, tested it locally, and obtained a return JSON message. Our next step is to host it on your Azure account so that it can be called on demand from the **API Management** portal or a logic app.

Publishing to Azure

In this section, we are going to host the function in Azure and make it accessible to your other projects:

1. On the **Azure** page, sign into Azure using your Microsoft account.

    A list of subscriptions related to your account will be displayed. Since I have an MSDN account, I will store my function here:

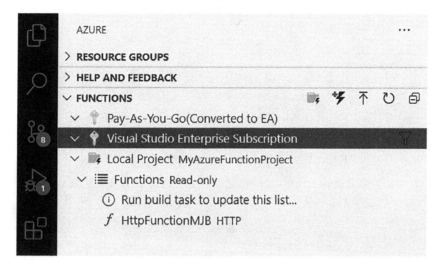

Figure 7.19 – Signing into Azure and viewing your list of subscriptions

2. Press the **Deploy to Function App** (**Upload**) button to start the wizard:

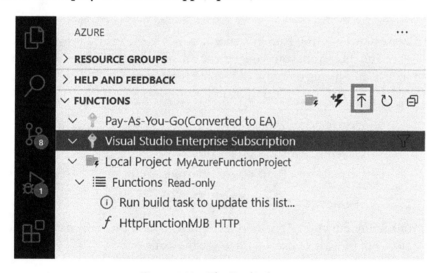

Figure 7.20 – The Deploy button

3. Select which project (folder) you wish to deploy:

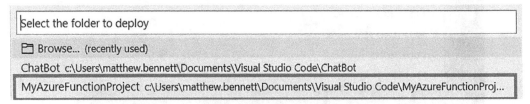

Figure 7.21 – Selecting your project to deploy

4. Next, choose which subscription is best for you (in my case, I will be using my MSDN subscription):

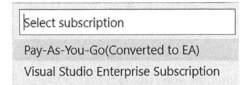

Figure 7.22 – Selecting the subscription that this project will be associated with

5. Select **Create new Function App in Azure...**, which is the easiest way to create a new Azure Function from your code. If you already have an Azure function and want to update an existing one, you can search for it here:

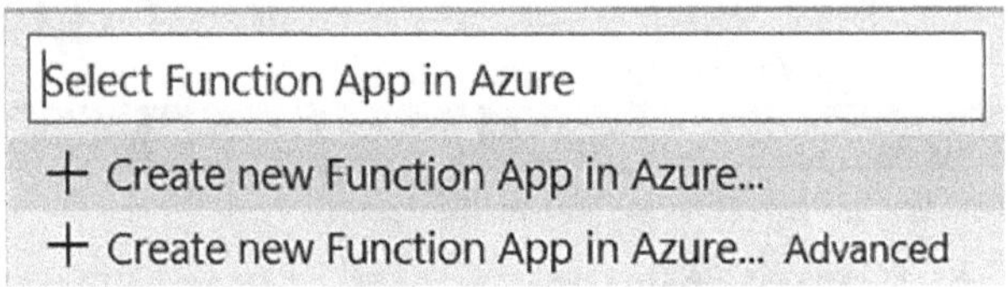

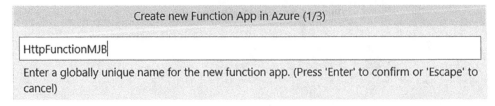

Figure 7.23 – Create new Function App in Azure…

6. Name your Azure Function App. It does not have to have the same name as the local project, but for ease of use, I tend to use the same one:

Create new Function App in Azure (1/3)

HttpFunctionMJB

Enter a globally unique name for the new function app. (Press 'Enter' to confirm or 'Escape' to cancel)

Figure 7.24 – Naming the Azure Function App

7. Select the version of .NET you used when creating the project:

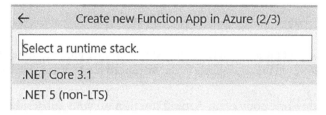

Figure 7.25 – Selecting the runtime stack

8. Next, select which Microsoft region you wish to use. As a UK resident, I tend to use UK West or UK South:

Figure 7.26 – Selecting your local data center

At this point, remember to check the legal geography of your code – publish only to a data center you are comfortable hosting in. Not all regions offer all the services you may require – check your service availability with Microsoft before committing to a region.

Tip

When working on **Production Enterprise Azure** resources, please bear the legal implications in mind as you may be restricted regarding which countries you can store your data in.

The project will be converted into an **Azure Function** and provisioned in your selected subscription.

> **Note**
>
> The wizard does not prompt you regarding which resource group to store the resource in. However, this is available in the **Advanced** mode of the installation.

You can only store one copy of an Azure Function on your subscription with the same name. You cannot have different instances of the function with the same name in different resource groups. For this reason, where a function needs to be shared across resource groups, it is a common practice to create a general or "core" resource group.

9. Once deployed, you will receive a message in Visual Studio Code to confirm this:

Figure 7.27 – Visual Studio Code completion message

10. Let's check this out in Azure. As you can see, using the basic wizard has created a resource group with the same name as our function:

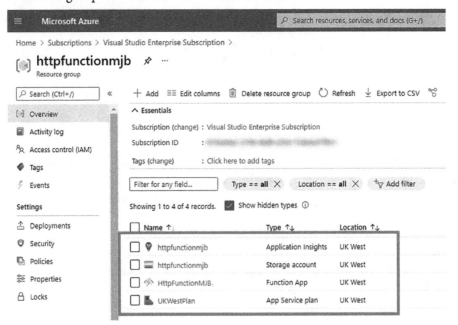

Figure 7.28 – Azure with a dedicated resource group for the function and its supporting objects

Finally, navigating to `https://httpfunctionmjb.azurewebsites.net/` will allow you to access the Azure cloud version of your function.

In this exercise, you created your first `Hello world` style basic function, which uses an input parameter. You tested it locally and published it to your Azure cloud.

In the next section, we will learn how to send data to an Azure function.

Sending data to an Azure Function from a logic app

Connecting an Azure function to the outside world is very easy. In this section, we will handle data input to the Azure function via an **HTTP request** trigger. The reason for this is that you might want to amend the data or perform calculations before sending the data into the function for processing.

Follow these steps to learn how to send data to an Azure function:

1. First, create a logic app, as detailed in the previous chapters. I have called mine `InputParamsLA`.

2. Set your trigger to be an HTTP request, either by using the template or creating a blank logic app first and then selecting the **Request** trigger, as detailed in previous exercises.

3. Copy the JSON message we are going to use as input to your clipboard:

   ```
   { "name": "Matthew" }
   ```

4. Open your trigger, select the **Use sample payload to generate schema** link, and paste the JSON message into the generator. A schema will be created for you:

   ```
   {
       "type": "object",
       "properties": {
           "name": {
               "type": "string"
           }
       }
   }
   ```

The input variables and field name (in this case, it is called name) must match the expected parameters within the Azure function. If you expand the input parameters, you will need to add these as parameters to the C# project and republish your function:

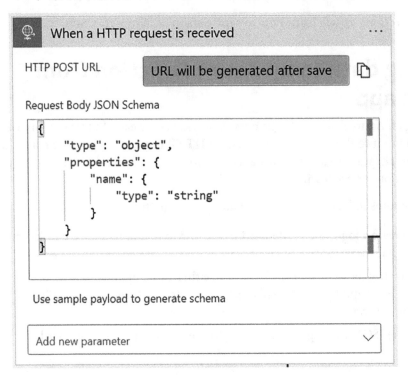

Figure 7.29 – The completed trigger with the correct schema

5. Below the trigger, add an action. From the **Dynamic** catalog, search for Azure function:

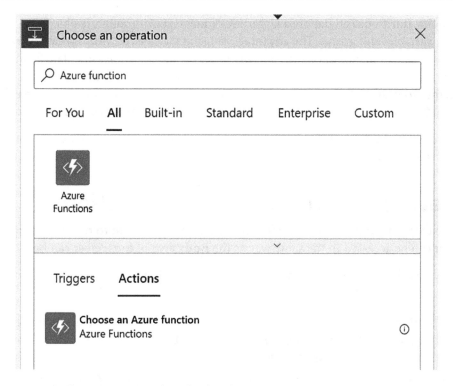

Figure 7.30 – Searching for the Choose an Azure Function action

6. When you select this action, all the Azure functions within the subscription will be accessible. Select **HttpFunctionMJB**.

    The function will now be displayed as our first action, but if you want to manipulate the input before you pass the data to the function, you should add additional steps between the trigger and the Azure Function action. In this exercise, we will use the direct input from the trigger without any changes.

7. Since we are only using the name parameter, select **name** from the Trigger section in the **Dynamic** content as our input parameter:

Figure 7.31 – Selecting name as the input parameter

More complex functions can handle a larger JSON message with multiple objects containing variables and arrays. The advantage of using JSON over XML is that you can keep the data type in its native format, and the function also uses the same data format – there is no need for data conversions from string into integer (for example). In this example, the **Body** area of the JSON message is sent to the function, which will parse the message and manage each component separately, then recombine a message for output.

So, we have called the Azure function, but how do we deal with the return output data? We will look at this in the next section.

Retrieving data from an Azure Function

To retrieve data from the function, the function needs a mechanism to return an output. The output can be accessed in the same way as the **Body** area of the trigger can be.

Here, we will look at how to refine the logic app to read and make sense of the output data from the Azure Function:

1. Continuing with our logic app, **add a new action** below the Azure function. From the **Dynamic** catalog, select **Response**. The default 200 response, which indicates a successful reply to the sender, will be sent.

2. In the **Body** parameter, select the body that is the output of the function. This will be sent back to the user.

    Again, if you need to manipulate the output, additional actions can be added between the Azure Function and the response. However, be mindful that the message will need to be parsed with a Parse JSON action first to reveal the separate components. The schema of the Parse JSON needs to match the output of the Azure Function:

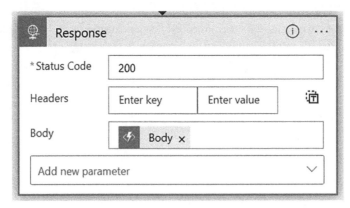

Figure 7.32 – Adding the Body message from the Azure function as the return to the user

3. The final message will read as follows (in my case):

```
Hello, Matthew. This HTTP triggered function executed successfully.
```

Figure 7.33 – The output return message

So far, you have managed to retrieve some output, process it, and return it to the caller (via a *Postman* or *Fiddler* app call) in a response.

Summary

In this chapter, we looked at how to use the Visual Studio Code application to create your first function. In our case, this was a C# project. Then, we connected to our Azure subscription, tested the project locally, and published the project to the cloud as an Azure function. After, we created a wrapper logic app to pass input data and return the output to the user.

In the next chapter, we are going to look at how to segment the logic app into logical areas, as well as how to perform the equivalent of try/catch actions to determine how to handle problematic code.

8
Scoping with Try/Catch Error Handling

As the complexity of the logic grows, it would be sensible to divide the flowchart into different sections. The **scope** feature allows you to do this, reducing clutter on the flowchart. Output from a scope can also be obtained for debugging purposes. The scope feature has a further use of being able to focus the developer's attention on problematic code. Output and error messages from this section can be obtained and debugged, with further remedial actions taken when errors do occur.

In this chapter, you will learn how to do the following:

- Create a series of scope sections to simplify the logic into higher levels, enabling the overall flowchart to be easier to understand

- Manipulate and move existing actions into a scope to contain data in a sectional way

- Examine a Try scope's output for debugging data

- Triage error data to ensure the logic is more robust by adding extra logic when things go wrong

Technical requirements

The following are the technical requirements for this chapter:

- JSONLint
- JSON Formatter
- JSON Schema tool
- OData site
- OData query reference
- Knowledge of XML and SQL queries

Creating a series of scope sections

As work on your logic app grows ever more complex, it's good practice to break your code into logical sections. This is determined by the object being tested, or the data being manipulated now. For example, you might want to look up a contact and then from this information obtain a list of the contact details for that person. From this, you may want to produce an array of the person's contact details. In this scenario, there are three clear sections to the logic app:

- Obtaining the correct person
- Obtaining this person's contact details
- Generating an array of contact details

Each of these sections can be made by using the **scope object**. Scoping has several uses, as we will discover in this chapter, but the most basic and obvious function is to break apart the logic app into high-level sections to make it easier for other developers to read and to understand what is happening.

This is the current high-level design for the logic app:

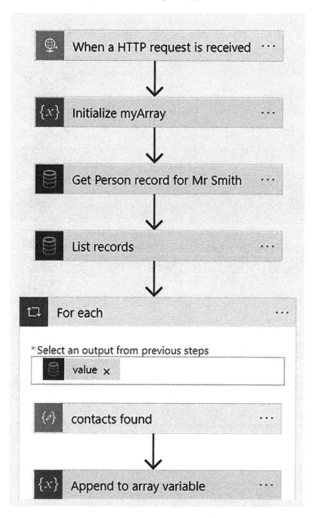

Figure 8.1 – Designing a logic app without scoping is difficult to understand

By creating scope sections and moving the actions within them, the high-level nature of the logic app design makes the design easier to understand:

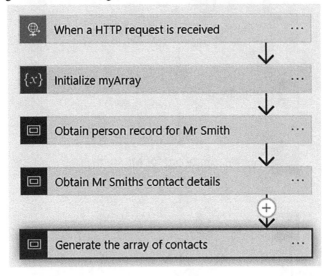

Figure 8.2 – The same logic app with scoping sections

Let's detail the logic app steps.

Here is the first section of the logic app:

Figure 8.3 – GetemailCRM1 section 1

Here is the second section of the logic app:

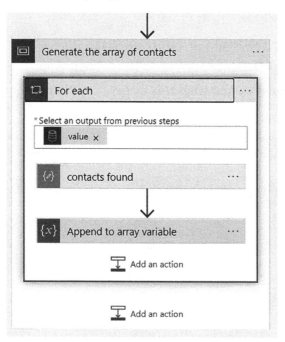

Figure 8.4 – GetemailCRM1 section 2

In this section, we have looked at creating high-level sections that can also be used as Try-Catch statements within your code. This is great for the initial high-level design of your logic app but also is also useful to catch errors within a section.

Manipulating and moving existing actions into a scope

Let's create the logic app together. We will first create scope sections and then will populate these with the key actions.

> **Note**
>
> As your CRM may be designed with different field names, entity names, and environment names, yours will not be an exact match, but you should be able to deduce similar fields in your system.

ur next exercise will show you how you can use scoping for greater control and analysis f your logic app.

Exercise – Creating the GetemailCRM1 logic app

Perform the following steps:

1. Create the logic app as detailed in earlier chapters.

2. On the **Logic Apps Designer** page, select **Blank Logic App**.

3. Select **HTTP request** as your trigger, as we have done in previous exercises.

    Your logic app should look like this:

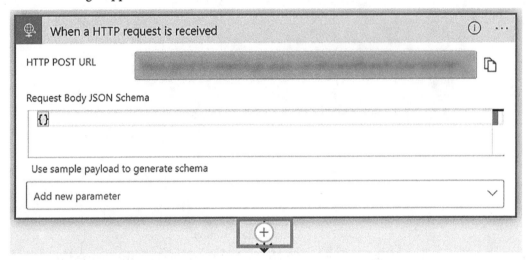

Figure 8.5 – Request HTTP trigger generated also showing the Add an action button

4. Press the **Insert a new step** button and from the drop-down list, select **Add an action**. Select **Initialize variable** from the **Variables** section in the catalog:

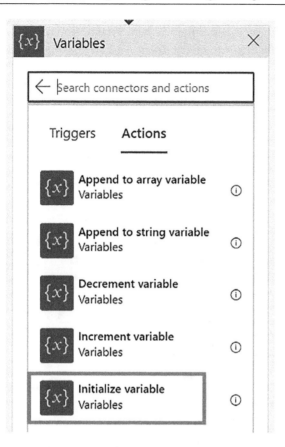

Figure 8.6 – Selecting Initialize variable

5. Name the array myArray and change the variable type to **Array**. Leave the initial value blank but use the more (**…**) button to rename the action:

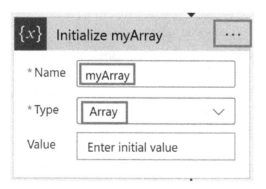

Figure 8.7 – myArray action correctly detailed and renamed

6. Below the array action, press either the **New step** button or the **Insert a new step** button and from the drop-down list select **Add an action** to open the catalog of actions.

    From the **Control** section of the catalog, select **Scope**:

Figure 8.8 – The Scope action in the Control section of the catalog

7. You will be presented with an empty **Scope** box. Repeat this action two further times.

8. Rename the scopes with a more sensible and easier-to-understand section name for each. This is again done by using the more (**…**) button, as we did previously in the exercise.

Your logic app should look like this:

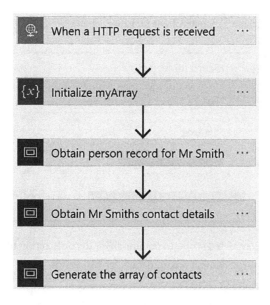

Figure 8.9 – Logic app with scope sections

You can choose to create the actions inside the scope or create them outside the scope and then drag and drop the action inside the expanded scope section.

Scope section 1

Perform the following steps:

1. Expand the scope.
2. We are going to find a specific person from your CRM. The person's Contact ID is already known to us, so we can use the GUID to find the record. Press the **Add an action** button to open the catalog. From the **Common Data Service** actions, select the **Get Record** action and populate it as follows:

A. **Environment: Test**

B. **Entity Name: Contacts**

C. **Item Identifier:** <Your person contact GUID for Mr. Smith>

Rename the action with a task-specific action name using the more (…) button, as before.

The completed first scope should look like this:

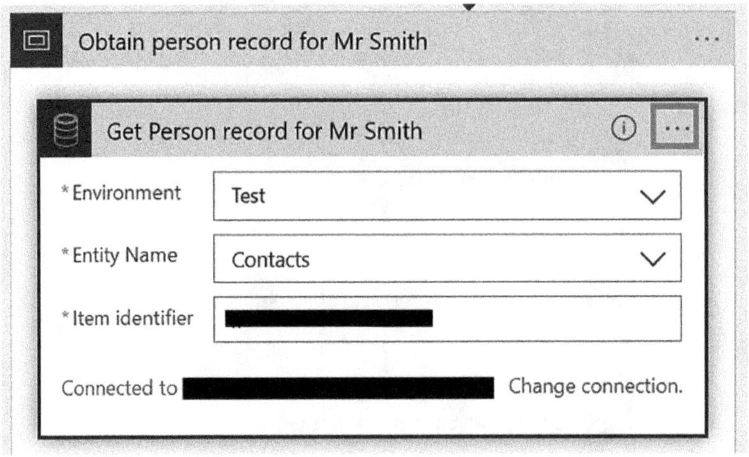

Figure 8.10 – Completed scope 1 contains a Get Records action to acquire
the contact record details for Mr. Smith

By doing this, you get the benefit of being able to examine the scope data for the whole section as well as specifically "drilling down" into the **Get Person record** action.

In the next section, we will look at how to set up the scope for the next section.

Scope section 2

Perform the following steps:

1. Expand the scope.

2. Add an action and, from the catalog, look for the **Common Data Service** action **List records**. Set the action to the following details:

   A. **Environment: Test**

   B. **Entity Name: Contact Types**

3. Add a new parameter and select **Filter query**. This will enable you to perform an OData query to obtain all the contacts related to Mr. Smith:

Filter Query: `contactid eq Contact`

> TIP
>
> On the preceding action, please ensure you select the **Contact ID** (logical name is **Contact**) that is coming from the **Get Person record for Mr Smith** action). Also, **contactid** is the physical field name within the **Contact Types** entity, and this may be a differently named field on your CRM.

If you want to, you can create the action outside of the scope, or between the scopes, then drag and drop the action into the scope.

The completed scope section 2 should look like this:

Figure 8.11 – Completed scope section 2

We now have a completed scope section 2. However, I want to just take a moment to think through the next section of the logic app.

Before we start to build the final scope section, let's just pause for a moment. We have one contact (Mr. Smith) who could have multiple **Contact Types** in the CRM as we may be holding his contact details as separate records. Scope section 1 will return one record, which is why we used the **Get Records** action. As there was potentially more than one **Contact Type** to find, we used a **List records** action. Scope Section 3 therefore needs to deal with multiple records.

Given the preceding condition, we will need to cycle through each returned record and add it in sequence to the array we are going to build. If we don't do this and carry on with the **Compose** action, well – which data element should we store?

If you do not add a **For each** action and wrap your subsequent actions inside it, Azure will do it for you as it realizes that we will be handling more than one return from the **List records**. It realizes this the moment you try to obtain fields from the **List records** action in either the **Append** or **Compose** actions.

Scope section 3

Let's assume we don't want to take the shortcut here and follow the normal procedure:

1. In scope section 3, click on **Add an action**. Select the **Control** section from the catalog but this time, select the **For each** action:

Figure 8.12 – Selecting the For each action

As you can see from the screenshot, we can select **For each**, but be careful! Microsoft regularly updates the catalog and names do change.

2. In the **Select an output from previous steps** field, select the **Value** field of the earlier **List records** action, from the **Dynamic content** catalog.

3. Select **Add an action** within the **For each** block. From the **Dynamic catalog**, in the **Data operations** section, select the **Compose** action.

    The **For each** value field is in fact an object representing the current record the **For each** action is iterating through. Within this, you can obtain the field data for this record. The same schema is used as with the **List records** action but notice that the path to the logical name will reference the **For each** item. The expression to obtain this data would be as follows:

    ```
    items('For_each'?['contactdetails'])
    ```

4. Below the **Compose** action, from the **Variables** section of the **Dynamic catalog**, select the **Append to array variable** action. Set the name of the array to be **myArray** (this is the only one available in the drop-down list) and with a **Value** of **Contact Details** as we did in the **Compose** action earlier.

5. Rename the action so that it is more meaningful and easier to understand.

Note that the default behavior of this action is to process all the records found at the same time, in parallel. However, we want to sequence and build an array here, so we need to process them in series (one at a time). To do this, we need to amend the **Concurrency** and **Parallelism** settings on the action:

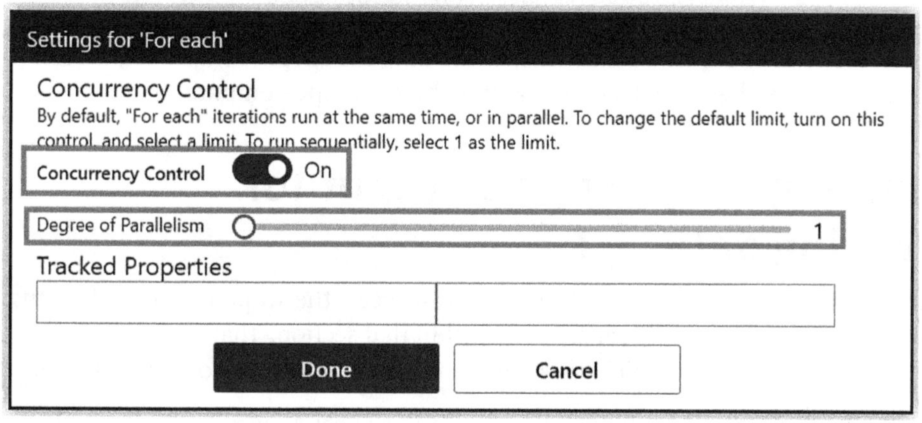

Settings for 'For each'

Concurrency Control
By default, "For each" iterations run at the same time, or in parallel. To change the default limit, turn on this control, and select a limit. To run sequentially, select 1 as the limit.

Concurrency Control   ● On

Degree of Parallelism   ○————————————————————————————————   1

Tracked Properties

Done   Cancel

Figure 8.13 – Setting the For each action to operate in series

The completed scope section 3 should look like this:

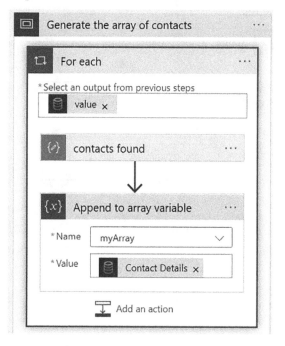

Figure 8.14 – Completed scope section 3

If you were to run your logic app, of course, your data may differ from mine. My "Mr Smith" has three contacts. These are two phone numbers and an email address. The resulting array pipes a text string we can analyze by using other logic or import into a new system.

My resulting array was as follows:

```
01906 231765|078714232456|marksmith75@test.com
```

As a result, the return value is a piped array containing the telephone number, mobile number, and email address. Let us now examine the Try scope's output.

Examining a Try scope's output for debugging data

One other advantage of using scopes is that you can access the scope's own result status to see whether there is any problematic code within that section. That is useful when you want to test a section of your logic app you are unsure about or think of as unreliable.

To simulate this, I've amended our exercise. Scope 3 has been moved to the top of the logic app and simply renamed **scope**, for clarity. Within the scope, I have added a **Terminate** action of **Failed** (this can be found in the **Control** section of the **Dynamic catalog**). The new scope now looks like this:

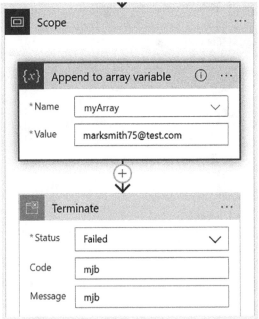

Figure 8.15 – The amended scope with a forced failure

When I run this, the **Terminate** action will force a failure at this point. As an action within the scope has failed, the entire scope will be marked as failed.

Failure is a good and useful process. Logic apps should be tested both for their success as well as how they behave when they do fail. For example, I set a `Boolean` field in **Dynamics**. How many different data responses can a `Boolean` field have? Any good mathematician will tell you that the answer is two: `true` and `false`. However, **Dynamics** uses trinary logic by including `null` as a value and for `null` to be the default. Had I not realized this, some records would have been left as `null` and some set to `false` in my logic. A later bulk update of the records based on this field would only have updated a small subset of the `false` records, ignoring the `null` records.

Triaging error data to ensure the logic is more robust

Now that we know that we can determine the status of a section of the logic app that might have failed, we can add control logic to send a message to the user alerting them of a problem.

As a cloud developer managing complex logic, I have to do this all the time. We have complex, closed systems that are not really meant to communicate with other systems but are using logic apps as an intermediary step to surface data and copy it over to other systems. Checks and balances take place within the logic app, but invariably users might miss important information such as item codes, or other key information that due to its omission means that the logic app cannot continue. Having a mechanism to catch these errors and immediately send a message to the user advising them that a problem has occurred will ensure that they can recheck their work and resubmit, rather than the lengthy process of raising **Service Desk** tickets and opening an investigation of the problem. If the user can simply try again, that must be the best option.

Exercise – Handling scope result messages

To determine the status of a scope, we can create a **condition check** immediately after the scope. The logic app would normally fail at the point of the failure, but handling the scope result, we can still take the opportunity to both perform *surgery* on the data and continue the logic app run, or to alert the user that a problem has occurred so that they can try again:

1. Create a **Condition** action below the scope you wish to test. Conditions are found within the **Control** section of the **Dynamic catalog**.

2. Set the condition to have two tests. We are going to test whether the result is either **Failed** or **Aborted**:

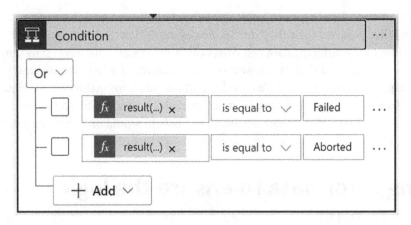

Figure 8.16 – Testing for a Failed or an Aborted scope result

The expression code you will need is as follows:

```
result('Scope')[0]['status']
```

This means the following:

A. Looking at the scope object's result status array, obtain the value stored in position 0.

B. In the **True** branch of the condition, add any code you want to take place because a failure has taken place:

Figure 8.17 – True condition branch contains your triage logic

3. In the **False** condition branch, continue with the logic app as normal as the scope has succeeded:

Figure 8.18 – False condition branch for "business as usual"

I tend to get my logic mixed up very easily. Some days, I will write conditions back to front (as to my mind this one appears). I am used to seeing the "true" path representing success, not as we have here, picking up on a failure.

> **Note**
>
> Please be careful, as reversing the *is equal to* operation to an *is not equal to* will not have the effect you might imagine. **True** and **False** condition branches have one flaw – they assume binary logic, not trinary. It is often better to test for `null` as well as `false` to ensure a complete dataset.

This brings us to the end of the exercise on handling scope result messages.

Summary

You must remember that when working as part of a team of developers, your code should be easy to read and make sense without reading too deeply. Sectioning your logic app by using the scope allows for two things – a high-level reading of the logic app from a design perspective, and the ability to triage based on the status result of a scope section in much the same way that the **TRY/CATCH** and **FINALLY** actions are used in C# programming to handle problem data.

In the next chapter, we are going to look at how we can call other logic apps at certain times. We can have dedicated, reusable logic apps that perform regular core functions. We will look at three ways to communicate between logic apps and the benefits/pitfalls of each method.

9

Sharing Data with Other Logic Apps and APIs

As logic apps grow ever more complex, we can build them with reusable code parts. Common, repeatable logic can be used time and again by a series of other parent logic apps. A parent logic app refers to the starting logic app, where the initial trigger is located. On the other hand, a **child** logic app refers to the logic app that data is passed to for further processing. Large logic sequences are often split into parent and child logic apps. As such, this chapter will look at how to link logic apps together and share data between them.

In this chapter, we will cover the following topics:

- Using a logic app action to call a child logic app
- Using an HTTP call to trigger a further logic app
- Using a request/response pair to share data between logic apps

Technical requirements

To work on this chapter, you will need the following:

- A web browser.

- An Azure subscription.

- A standard Azure logic app containing a trigger of your choice to start the logic app (commonly, this is a recurrence, or an HTTP request trigger).

Using a logic app action to call a child logic app

As your logic develops, you might notice that certain sections need to be called multiple times, or that they might need to be called by several logic apps that are similar. The term **orchestrator** refers to a logic app that will take a trigger action and, depending on what logic is required, route the data message to the appropriate child logic app for the message to be dealt with correctly and for the correct fields to be populated.

Let's look at a real-life example. I am taking data from an old, closed system that does not contain any **Web APIs** (web-based RESTful web programming interfaces) that can be used to send data or a direct link that will allow me to obtain data in Azure. I do some **Read APIs** that allow me to obtain data, but not the other way around. By writing a C# app that will query the closed system's audit logs, I might not be able to get to the actual data, but I can understand which action has just taken place and from there, I can make a **GET API** call to obtain the data.

My data from the C# app was sent to Azure in the form of a JSON message that looked something like this:

```
{
    "Date": "25/2/21",
    "Time": "09:15:00",
    "Source": "LegacySystem",
    "ContactID": "12345",
    "Action": "Contact Details added"
}
```

This tells me that on `LegacySystem`, at the given date and time, a `Contact Details` line was added to contact `12345`.

The C# app would check the legacy system's audit log and poll for messages regularly. Then, it would send each as a series of messages to the trigger URL for my **gateway** logic app:

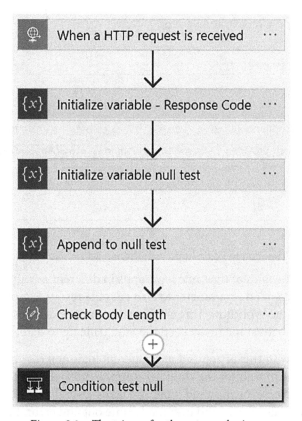

Figure 9.1 – The trigger for the gateway logic app

The gateway app reads the message and checks that the message is not malformed, empty, or missing any data (such as `ContactID`). Then, it checks the audit action against a SQL table that contains a list of audit actions and the trigger URL for the action's respective logic app.

Finally, an HTTP POST action is used to resend the message to the correct logic app for processing.

In my first version of this logic app, I used a logic app action step to call the logic app in question. My first attempt had a list of logic app names be used against the **Audit** action from the legacy system. By passing the appropriate name to the section marked with the tags in the following screenshot, you can see that the message is passed to different logic apps based on the **Audit** action:

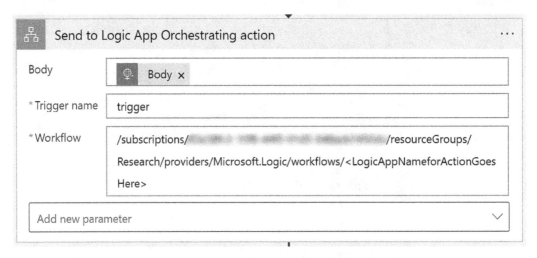

Figure 9.2 – The Send to Logic App Orchestrating action step (note the tag)

In a later revision, I had copies of the same logic apps in different resource groups. I extended the table and added a parameter to also pass the resource group name to where the word *Research* is in the Workflow. This is OK until someone decides to recreate and rename a logic app – you must manually keep the SQL table up to date.

One further drawback with this action is that the parent logic app (the gateway logic app featured here) will pause to wait for the child logic app to finish. If there is an error that causes the logic app to freeze, or the child logic app takes several minutes to complete, the parent logic app will also freeze and eventually time out and error. I found this to be somewhat misleading and irritating.

To combat this, there are several different ways we can call a child logic app. Some affect the wait timer that's used by the parent logic app, though some do not. We will examine each of these in the next section.

> **Tip**
>
> When working with logic app action calls such as these, if you have a logic app of the same name in multiple different resource groups, all of them will be presented when you choose which logic app you want to action. It can be difficult to select the right one. If you have chosen the wrong one, check the path in Code View; you will notice that you can change the resource group folder to pick up the correct one.

Using an HTTP call to trigger a further logic app

As I mentioned previously, the initial method of using a child logic app action is, in my opinion, an inefficient solution. The replacement is to amend the SQL table so that it holds the trigger URLs for every logic app against their audit action. This way, I can send an HTTP POST call to fire the appropriate logic app, like so:

ID	Action	URL
1	Create Contact	https://xxxxx
2	Update Contact	https://yyyyy

Figure 9.3 – URLs used to fire a logic app

This table is used to determine which URL is used to fire the appropriate logic app:

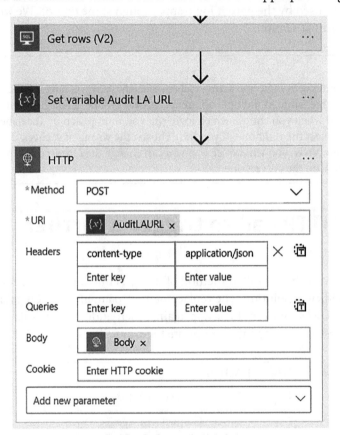

Figure 9.4 – Obtaining the action URL and dynamically using this to forward the HTTP POST method

By doing this, we have control over which logic app receives the message. Changing the name of a logic app will have no impact as the trigger URL that's used is not the name. However, recreating or cloning the child **action** logic app will produce a different URL as trigger URLs are randomized when the logic app is first saved.

One major benefit of using this method is that it is a *fire and forget* method – the message is sent and there is no need for the gateway logic app to wait for a response.

> **Tip**
>
> Set the **Retry Policy** setting of this action and change it from **Default** to **None**. The reason for this is that you only want to send one message to the child logic app. If you forget to do this, the child logic app could potentially receive four copies of the message (the default retry count is four).

So, by doing this, our parent logic app is not timing out if the child logic app takes too long to respond or fails to complete. However, communication is one way. In the next section, we will look at how to provide return information to the parent logic app.

Using a request/response pair to share data between logic apps

There are times when the opposite is true – you want to send a message and you are expecting a return in good time. Here, you may just want a child logic app at the heart of it all, or an Azure Function as the engine for your processing. In my example and sticking with contacts, now I know that an action has taken place, and which **Contact** this affects, I have created a **GetContact** logic app that will perform an HTTP API POST call back to the legacy system to obtain the contact records. From here, I can pick out the new field, reformat the data, and then pass it into my new system (in my case, the contact's record in D365).

In the middle of my child logic app, which is designed to create a contact detail line, I have an HTTP action to the **GetContact** logic app. This performs the record lookup in the legacy system:

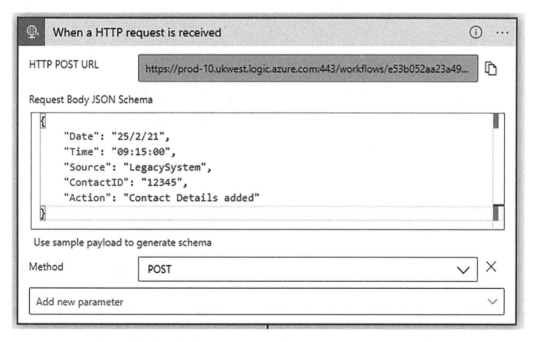

Figure 9.5 – The GetContact logic app has a request for its trigger action

In the **GetContact** logic app, at the very end, there is a **Response** action, which is used to return the output to the calling parent logic app:

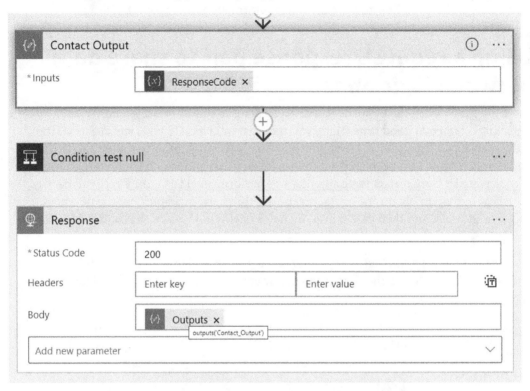

Figure 9.6 – The GetContact logic app ends by sending the response back

Here, the 200 **Response** action will provide output back to the parent logic app, where the output can be parsed and used in further logic in the main (the parent) logic app.

However, there are different response actions you may wish to consider. These will be covered in the next section.

Status codes

It is worth mentioning that you can only send one response back. If you need to process the data and then return it to the parent logic app, you must add status 200 (everything is OK) as the **Response** action. Then, the message can be parsed and used by your parent logic app. However, the parent logic app will be waiting for a response and if one is not received within a good amount of time (2 minutes, based on the current Azure configuration), then the parent logic app will produce an error.

However, if you want the parent logic app to send its message and not monitor how the child logic app is doing, you can send a 202 return message in a parallel branch at the start of the logic app. This effectively tells the parent to stop waiting for a return message and continue. You might like to leave a status message, as shown here:

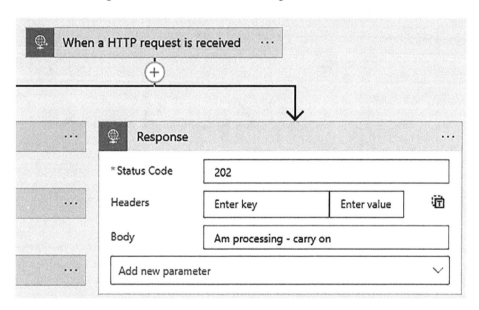

Figure 9.7 – Logic app sending a 202 response for the parent logic app to continue

So, by adding either a 200 response or a 202 response, you can control whether the parent logic app will wait for the child logic app to complete.

Default tries on an action

Any logic app action that calls for data will have a retry policy that explains the behavior of the action when a success message is not returned, along with the expected data. Logic app calls to the Dataverse (Common Data Service), SQL queries, or API calls all operate using web technologies, so standard HTTP error codes are anticipated. Codes such as a 408, 429, or 500 error will trigger the logic app to try again and repeat the request, should the **Retry Policy** option be set to require this:

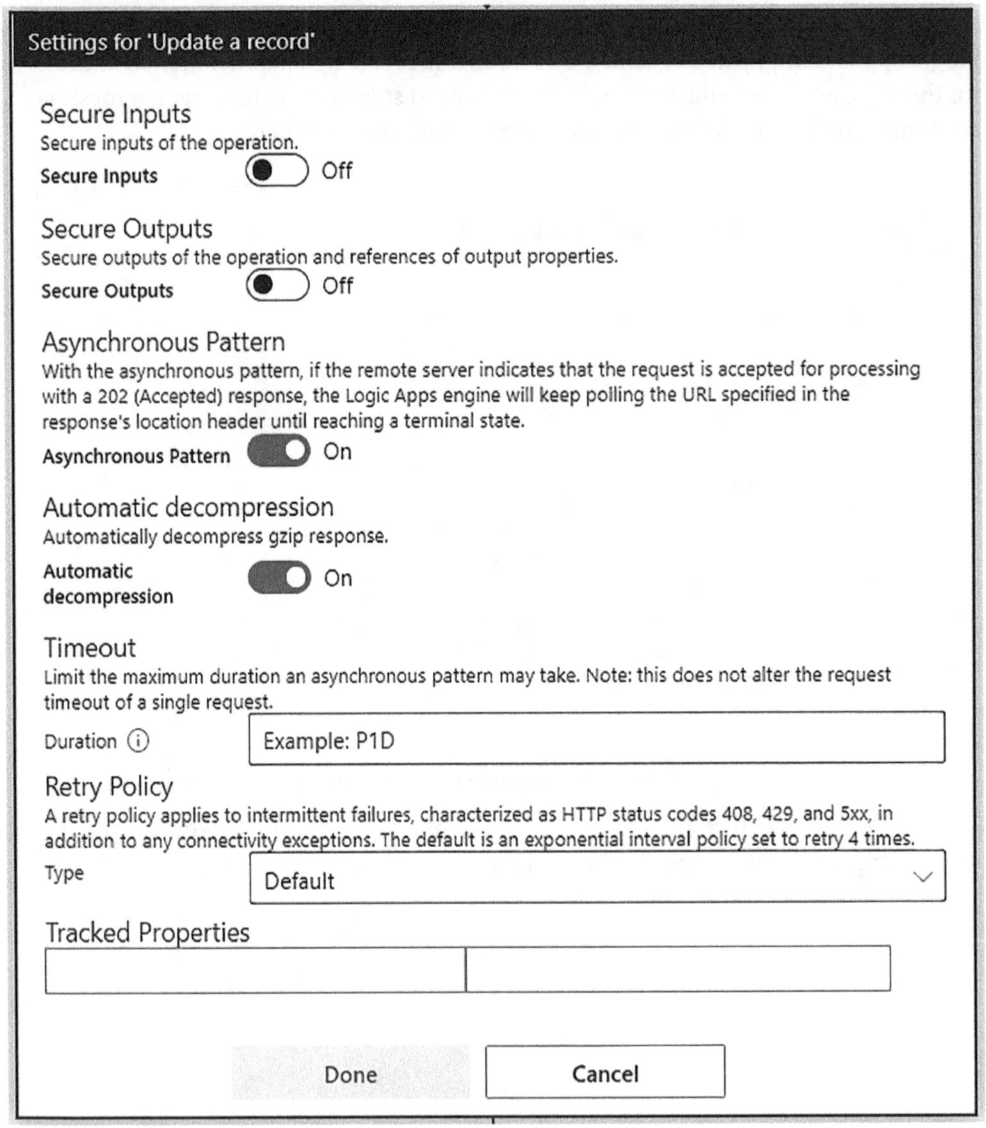

Figure 9.8 – Retry Policy is set to Default

A 408 error is a *request timeout*. The logic app has waited for a long period (typically, 2 minutes) and has expected to hear an answer by this point, so it is now requesting that the connection be closed.

A 429 error is a *rate-limiting* error – there have been too many requests to this resource at this point, so no further requests will be accepted until traffic has been reduced. Sending a message during a 429 period will mean that the request will be denied until the server can accept new requests.

A 500 error is a more severe error. It identifies that the resource you are trying to access is not working. It may be that a web server is stuck or powered down, or that a web app that drives a website has broken and needs to be restarted. Clearly, the resource is unable to accept the request at this point.

The default for all Azure Logic Apps actions is for them to be retried four times. Each try is a separate handshake event – the logic app will establish a connection to the endpoint first, send the message, then read the response before closing the connection. Should that process fail, the logic app will try again.

Then, you must think about what you are going to do when the message is not received. You might choose to create a *fail branch*, in which we take remedial action, or attempt to retrieve the data another way using a different resource (such as a backup server or a read-only copy of the database contained in a data warehouse, rather than making a call to the live database). If we are going to allow the logic app to fail at this point, we need to think about whether there will be any knock-on effects, considering that there could be other logic that may not have been actioned, given that the logic app has stopped at the point of failure.

The impact of losing messages

If you are planning to use the **HTTP POST** action, please bear in mind that this is different from a **Request/Response** action in that **HTTP POST** sends the message but does not read the output (it operates on the *fire and forget* principle). Therefore, if you are sending to a resource that could be busy, will the message be actioned? If the resource is turned off, do you have a mechanism to be able to rerun the message at a later point? Here, setting the retry policy to the default (four tries) when sending a Web API message that inserts a record into a database would not be a good idea as the HTTP call could be sent four times. The record you are trying to add will effectively be added to the database four times!

For this reason, when using HTTP calls to keep systems in sync, I always set **Retry Policy** to **None**:

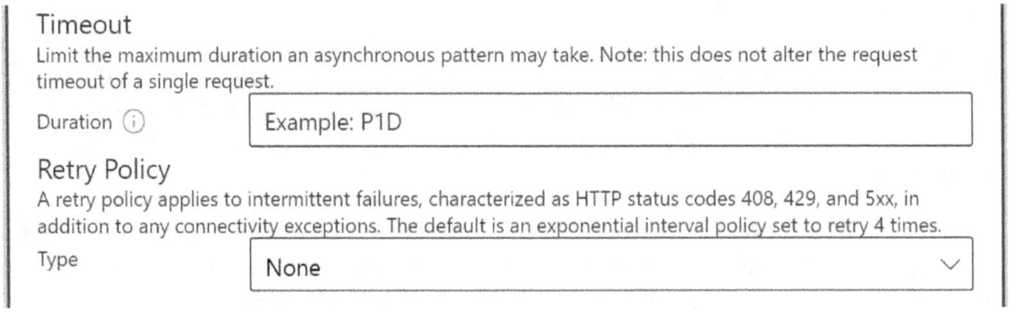

Timeout
Limit the maximum duration an asynchronous pattern may take. Note: this does not alter the request timeout of a single request.
Duration
Example: P1D
Retry Policy
A retry policy applies to intermittent failures, characterized as HTTP status codes 408, 429, and 5xx, in addition to any connectivity exceptions. The default is an exponential interval policy set to retry 4 times.
Type
None

Figure 9.9 – Setting Retry Policy to None

Therefore, by setting the policy to none, we can avoid additional and unwanted duplicate messages being sent to our resource.

Trigger IDs

A logic app will start to process data when the trigger condition has been met. However, this trigger can only be set to start the logic app (referred to as **firing**) if any specific requirements in the **Trigger** settings are also met. Here are two examples of where you could restrict the firing of a logic app:

- The filter field has not been updated. Here, we have a Dataverse (Common Data Service) standard trigger action, such as *Update a row*:

When a Tenancy record is updated
* Environment
Development
* Table Name
Tenancies
* Scope
Organization
Column Filters Item - 1
statuscode

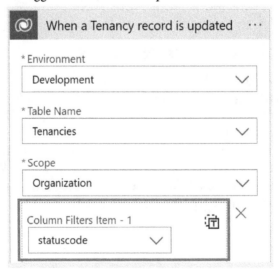

Figure 9.10 – The Column Filters parameter restricts when a logic app fires

In the preceding example, the logic app will only fire when a change has been made to the **statuscode** field on the record. If the user saves other changes, these will be ignored, and the logic app will not fire. This is an incredibly useful trick to ensure that logic app integration or processing the D365 record will only work when certain conditions have been met. In the process of creating a **Tenancy** record, the user will save multiple times as they progress through the various stages of the form. In my real-life example, I have included a **ready for integration** true/false toggle and set **Column Filters** to focus on this field. When the toggle is changed, the trigger will be successful, and the logic app will fire. By doing this, redundant saves in the CRM can be ignored.

- Adding a **Trigger Condition**. In the following example, I have a series of trigger conditions to bypass a problem. The owner of the CRM record is a service account. The record was added to the D365 CRM database as part of a bulk addition process from an older system I am now integrating with. The owner has not been changed to a user account, and I have many thousands of records in this condition. I have two-way integration in place, watching this field. I want to avoid the situation where adding a record to the CRM will trigger the logic app, which is managing the older system, to think that this is a new record and try readding this record to the older system, as per the following diagram:

Figure 9.11 – Two-way integration in place

The problem I was facing was that when I created a record in D365, the logic app would integrate the record into the legacy system. When the record was saved on the legacy system, the change was noted in the audit log. My audit tracking program noted the new record, and this fired a JSON message to Azure, stating that a new record had been saved in the legacy system. This fired **Create logic app**, which attempted to read the same record to D365. I was caught in an endless loop. To break this, I checked that a condition was in place (in the case of the following listed record, this is a **Contact** record, which must contain a link to a **Tenancy** record):

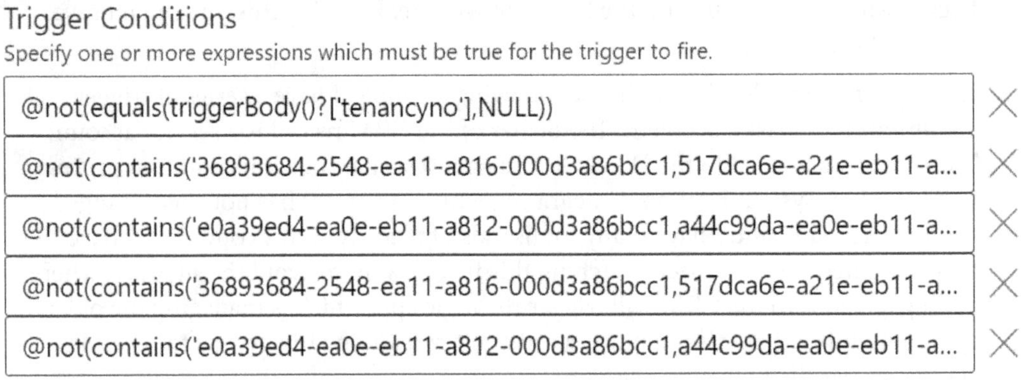

Trigger Conditions
Specify one or more expressions which must be true for the trigger to fire.

@not(equals(triggerBody()?['tenancyno'],NULL))	✕
@not(contains('36893684-2548-ea11-a816-000d3a86bcc1,517dca6e-a21e-eb11-a...	✕
@not(contains('e0a39ed4-ea0e-eb11-a812-000d3a86bcc1,a44c99da-ea0e-eb11-a...	✕
@not(contains('36893684-2548-ea11-a816-000d3a86bcc1,517dca6e-a21e-eb11-a...	✕
@not(contains('e0a39ed4-ea0e-eb11-a812-000d3a86bcc1,a44c99da-ea0e-eb11-a...	✕

Figure 9.12 – Trigger Conditions to restrict when a logic app fires

What we are saying here is that **Trigger Conditions** occur in the following situations:

- When there is a tenancy number on the record
- When the owner of the record is not a service account

Both conditions need to be met for the logic app to be fired.

The **Trigger history** list can be found on the **Overview** page, with the statuses detailing whether the logic app fired:

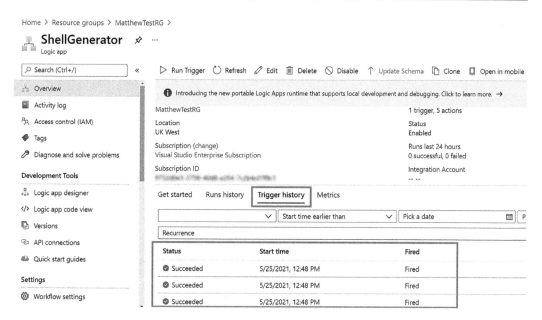

Figure 9.13 – Trigger history on the Overview page listing fired runs

So, by using the **Trigger history** list, we can call a specific firing by triggering the GUID or by filtering to a specific date and time.

Run IDs

Every logic app run also has a unique GUID. Sadly, this is not the same GUID as the trigger GUID, but the same user experience is presented to us – we can search for a specific run by GUID or filter to a specific date and time. This allows us to then analyze the run, explore the data that's been gathered, and spot any errors that may have occurred. As a developer, I spent a lot of my time having to backtrack through a logic app run to obtain IDs or key data, as well as to troubleshoot where issues had occurred.

One extremely useful feature is the ability to resubmit a run. You should use this when you have made a minor correction and wish to update an existing record. However, you should resubmit with caution if you are resubmitting a run from a logic app that's been used for integration purposes – this may have unintended effects and cause duplicate records to be created:

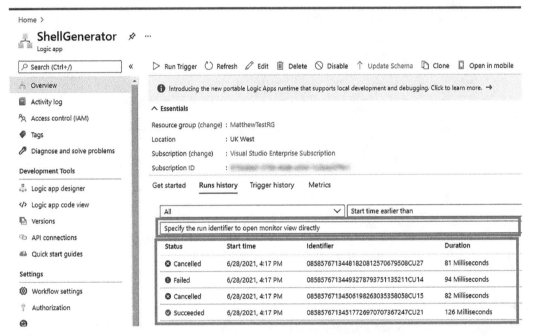

Figure 9.14 – Trigger history on the Overview page listing fired runs

Therefore, you can locate an existing run and resubmit it to update the record as needed.

> **Tip**
> Consider creating a parent logic app that locates a bulk number of records and a child logic app, which performs the core operations on each record found.

This brings us to the end of our discussion regarding sharing data with other logic apps.

Summary

This has been a short but concise chapter that has explained how to communicate between logic apps. We looked at the idea of an orchestrator – a central gateway in which you can receive messages and then reroute them for further processing. We considered how the parent and child logic apps communicate and looked at the traditional logic app action step as opposed to an HTTP action step. We then considered using a SQL table to index the audit actions in our message from our legacy system. We can then use this table to determine which logic app the message needs to be passed to.

After, we refined the HTTP POST action from the initial HTTP action step, which was very much like the one-way *fire and forget* principle and compared this to the request/ response actions. These work as a pair that receives an HTTP message and processes it within the logic app. At the end of the logic app, we send a message containing the output back to the parent logic app for further processing.

Controlling how messages are sent between logic apps is a very important consideration and can ensure that your Azure space remains well managed.

In the next chapter, we are going to revisit the logic app creation wizard with one important consideration – the use of Log Analytics, which is Azure's auditing system. Finally, we will create a management report and use it to check on failed runs, and then use this report to rerun failed runs in bulk.

10
Monitoring Logic Apps for Management Reporting

This chapter is designed to walk you through the Logic Apps creation wizard and to explain how Log Analytics is used to produce real-time reporting on resource group objects, providing a holistic overview of logic health within the monitored environment. By doing this, the developer can easily track errors in the logic, how often the problem is occurring, and where the fault is located.

The chapter will cover the following main topics:

- Using the Log Analytics workspace
- Walking through the wizard to create your first logic app
- Creating a management report and navigating it to find an error
- Working with Azure PowerShell for bulk operations

Technical requirements

For this chapter, you will need the following:

- A compatible browser such as Chrome or Edge
- The PowerShell console (default installed in Windows 10)
- The PowerShell ISE (also installable with Windows 10)

You will also need to install the Azure PowerShell module, which can be done via the `Install-Module` command.

Using the Log Analytics workspace

As your portfolio of logic apps grows, you will encounter a situation where some logic apps will fail due to poor data or poor logic. As you refine these, over time, you may wish to be alerted on the status of these logic apps, how many times they have run, which errors are the most common, and bulk rerun failed logic apps where you have identified the fault and are able to do so, rather than selecting them manually and triaging each in turn from within the Logic Apps overview page.

Exercise – creating your Log Analytics workspace

A Log Analytics workspace is a suite of queries that are automatically applied to audit data accessible from logic apps and other auditable resources. A workspace is a management tool that produces details and summary reports out of the box to show you the health of your resources. They can be used to show specific points in your logic that are flawed, or the data issues that are causing your resources to fail. They are an essential tool for Azure environment management.

The benefit of this action would be creating a management dashboard where you can have a high-level overview of your resource group over a given time. You can also "drill down" into specific errors and find out quickly why a run failed.

Follow the given steps to create your Log Analytics workspace:

1. Navigate to `portal.azure.com`.
2. From the home page, navigate to the resource group you wish to monitor. For me, this is **MatthewTestRG**.

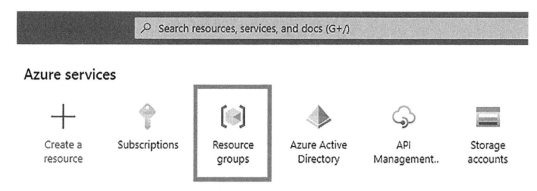

Azure services

+	**🔑**	**[◀]**	**🔺**	**☁**	**▤**
Create a resource	Subscriptions	Resource groups	Azure Active Directory	API Management..	Storage accounts

Recent resources

Figure 10.1 – The Azure portal home page, selecting Resource groups

3. From the **Resource group** page, which lists the resource groups available, we select the **MatthewTestRG** resource group.

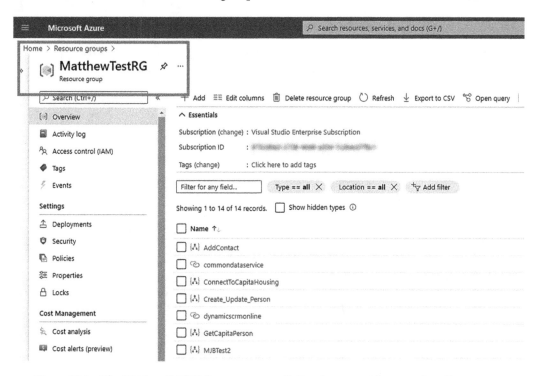

Figure 10.2 – The MatthewTestRG Resource group listing the current (not monitored) resources

4.   To add a new resource to this group, click the **+Add** button.

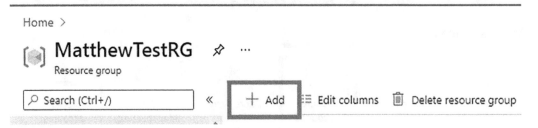

Figure 10.3 – Adding a new resource to this group

5.   In the **Create a resource** catalog, search for log analytics and select the **Log Analytics Workspace** tile.

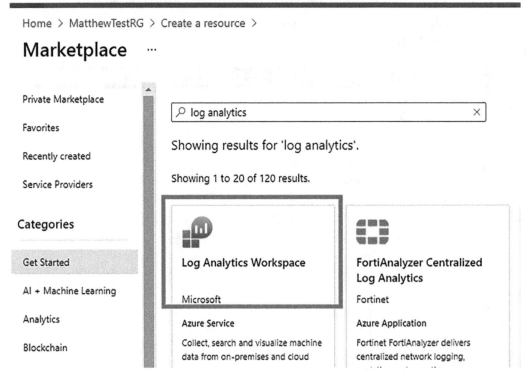

Figure 10.4 – Selecting the Log Analytics Workspace object

6. Click the **Create** button on the tile and from the drop-down list, select **Log Analytics Workspace**.

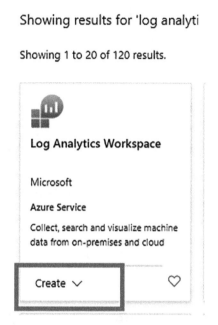

Figure 10.5 – Creating the Log Analytics workspace for this resource group

By doing this, a generic workspace will be created. This will contain an overview of all the logic apps where integration has been enabled. You will be able to also view a summary of passed/failed logic apps over time and see a list of common problems you may have.

> **Tip**
> You can only have one Log Analytics workspace per resource group.

7.   On the **Create Log Analytics workspace** form, please use the following details:

A. In the **Project details** section, enter the following:

B. **Subscription**: **Visual Studio Enterprise Subscription** (or your equivalent subscription).

C. **Resource group**: **MatthewTestRG**

In the **Instance details** section, enter the following:

A. **Name**: **MatthewRGLAW**

B. **Region**: **UK West**

Here is the completed form:

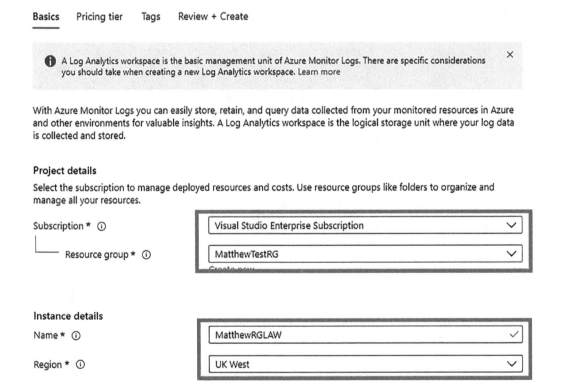

Figure 10.6 – Completing the Log Analytics workspace creation form

With this, you will be able to create your unique dashboard. Remember that these are customizable to a point, but the out-of-the-box graphics are very helpful.

> **Tip**
>
> The resource group you choose to monitor should be the same resource group you are going to monitor. However, some developers prefer to create a dedicated **management resource group** and place all workspaces into this central repository. Both methods are okay and will not affect performance.

8. While we can add tags and amend the pricing tier, for standard use, the preceding settings will suffice. Click **Review + Create** to continue to create the workspace.

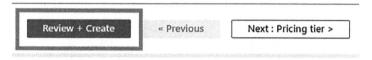

Figure 10.7 – Selecting the Review + Create button

We'll now progress to the next stage, where Azure will check for errors and omissions.

9. On the **Review + Create** tab, validation will check that your details are correct.

Figure 10.8 – Review + Create validation has passed

At this point, presuming there are no omissions, the validation will pass.

In my case, I have created a management dashboard that uses the Log Analytics log data to explain to me where each logic app is failing or having difficulty in my resource group. It took some time (several minutes and up to 1 day) before the log was ready to be processed and calculated.

Log Analytics has a query feature that allows you to look for specific records and events. There are also multiple template queries you can use to get started, but for the purposes of this chapter, we are going to focus on using Log Analytics invisibly to create a management dashboard.

10. If you need to amend anything, use the << **Previous** button.

Figure 10.9 – To proceed, use either the Create or << Previous button

11. The deployment will be in progress for up to 1 minute, depending on resources and availability. Once completed, click the **Go to resource** button to jump to the **Overview** page of your management workspace.

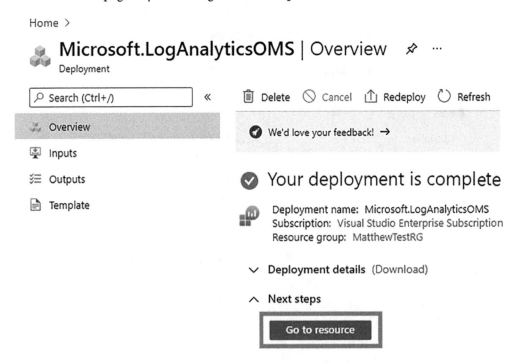

Figure 10.10 – The Go to resource button at the end of the creation wizard

The **Overview** page looks like the Logic Apps overview page, but with a few noticeable differences. You will notice that in section 1 – **Connect a data source**, you can connect to a variety of other resources, such as virtual machines, Windows, and Linux Agents (such as daemons), existing Azure Activity logs, storage account logs, and **System Center Operations Manager (SCOM)**, which is an essential infrastructure management tool. This can be helpful if you are considering a hybrid infrastructure and want to report on alerts from your on-premises system or pass on alerts from the Azure cloud to your on-premises network.

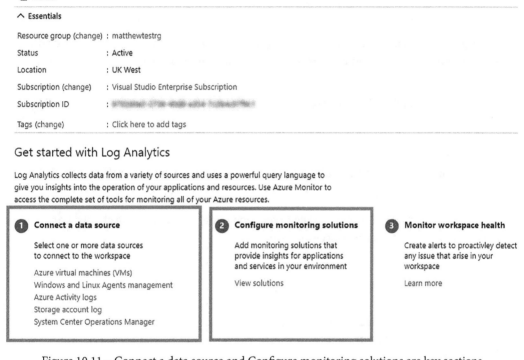

Figure 10.11 – Connect a data source and Configure monitoring solutions are key sections

12. For now, we are going to use section 2 – **Configure monitoring solutions** > **View solutions** to open the management dashboard.

> **Tip**
>
> Oh, that's disappointing. When I view the solution, I get a blank screen. The reason is that, up to now, none of our resources have a Log Analytics connection in the resource itself (when you first create the resource, you are prompted in the creation form as to whether you want to use Log Analytics, and up to this point we have not).
>
> Secondly, the subscription itself needs to allow for Log Analytics. This can be done by connecting the subscription to the Azure Activity log.

As a result of this exercise, you have created a Log Analytics workspace; however, we still must connect your subscription or resources to it. This will be done in the next exercise.

Exercise – connecting your subscription to enable Log Analytics

To use Log Analytics, Azure needs to know which account to use to pay for the additional activity. Creating logs puts additional demand on the Azure subscription. Here is how we enable Log Analytics:

1. From the **Log Analytics workspace Overview** page, select **Azure Activity Logs** from the **Connect a data source** section.

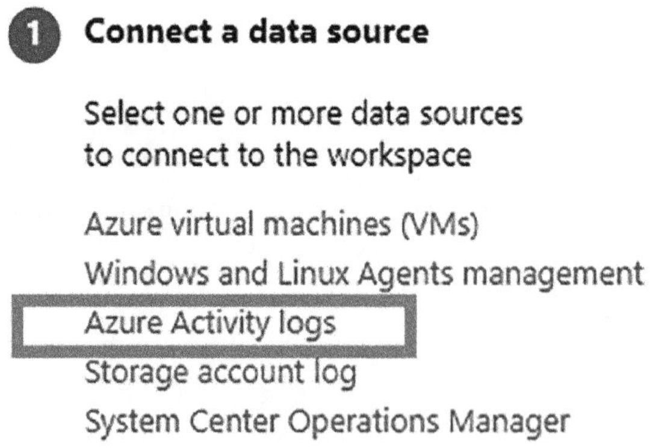

1 Connect a data source

Select one or more data sources
to connect to the workspace

Azure virtual machines (VMs)

Windows and Linux Agents management

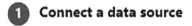

Storage account log

System Center Operations Manager

Figure 10.12 – Connecting the Azure Activity logs to the workspace

2. From the **Azure Activity log** page, select the **Subscription** option you wish to use to pay for this service. In my case, this is **Visual Studio Enterprise Subscription** (my MSDN account).

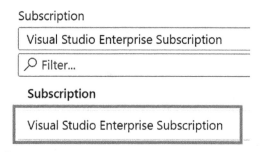

Subscription

Visual Studio Enterprise Subscription

🔎 Filter...

Subscription

Visual Studio Enterprise Subscription

Figure 10.13 – Connecting my subscription to the workspace

3. Also on the **Azure Activity log** page, click on the **Status** row to change the connection status.

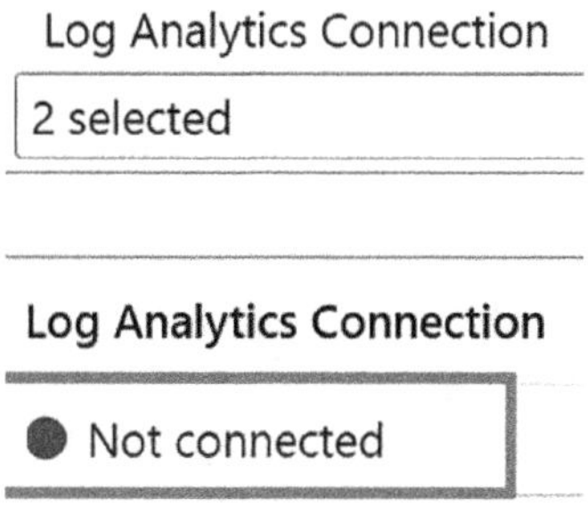

Log Analytics Connection

2 selected

Log Analytics Connection

● Not connected

Figure 10.14 – Click on the connection status, not the more button to set the connection

4. On the **Connect** page, we can see the current connection status in detail. Here, clicking the **Connect** button will enable the connection to your subscription.

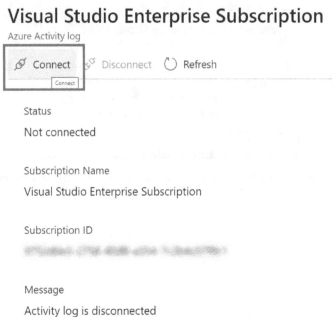

Fig 10.15 – The Connect page with the Connect / Disconnect buttons

After a few moments, you will receive a notification message to confirm that the subscription is now connected. Charges will now apply to this subscription.

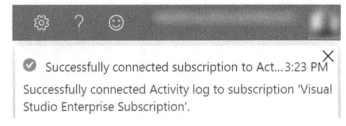

Figure 10.16 – The "successfully connected subscription" message

However, we now need a logic app to test this resource. In the next section, we will look at how the workspace works using my main workspace from a different resource group, but later in this chapter, we will provide some data for this workspace.

Using the dashboard

Eventually, you want a high-level overview that shows how many logic apps have fired within a given period. Also, you'll want to focus on how many have failed and need further action. This figure illustrates the high-level donut chart:

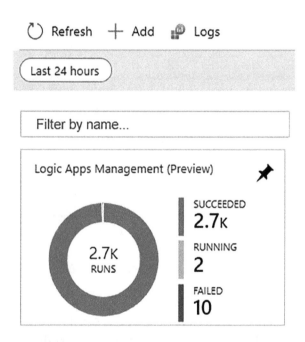

Figure 10.17 – The high-level donut summary tile

By drilling into this tile, we get a management report with data from a given period split into three sections:

- Logic app runs by **SUCCEEDED**, **RUNNING**, and **FAILED** states: This graphic is a repeat of the high-level tile we are first presented with when we open the Log Analytics workspace.

- **LOGIC APP RUNS BY STATUS**: This is a cumulative score of runs that have **Succeeded**, have **Failed**, or are **Running**, and then a total count (**All**) for that period. This is expressed as a line graph against time.

Figure 10.18 – Logic app runs by status

The graph therefore shows the amount of succeeded and failed runs over time. This is useful to show whether your logic apps are well written and meet the data requirements you are attempting to meet.

> **Tip**
> At the time of writing, there is a formatting issue on this page when rendered using Google Chrome. Notice that the table is drawn over the chart.

- **ACTIONS AND TRIGGERS BY ERROR CODE**: This section lists specific points of failure within the logic app, the type of error encountered, and a count of the number of times this occurred within the given period. This will help you to understand which logic is problematic, or not working as expected, or failing due to the type of data, or a lack of data being passed at this point.

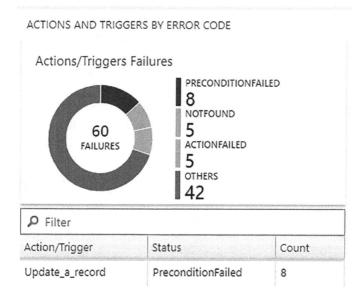

Figure 10.19 – Logic app runs by error code

This report also has many benefits in that you can filter it to specific errors. Also, by clicking on the failed runs on the middle (second) tile, you can obtain a table of failed logic app runs for a specific logic app. From here, you can bulk rerun these if required. This will be described in the *Creating a management report and navigating it to find an error* section of this chapter.

Walking through the wizard to create your first logic app

Although we briefly looked at this wizard in a previous chapter, you can only set whether a logic app will be monitored by the Log Analytics feature at the outset when you first create the logic app. (There may be a PowerShell script you can use to alter this afterward, but the easiest way if you do forget to do this is to clone your logic app, or manually re-create it, set the feature in the creation wizard, then copy the logic app back in your code before deleting the old version.)

What I propose we do is an exercise to make a logic app that will be used to demonstrate the different action states. Think of this as a problem logic app that needs your attention. To make this, we're going to make the logic app equivalent of the *Cup and Ball* game (the Shell game).

The Shell game is a game of chance where a pearl is placed under a shell (or a ball is placed under a cup). The cups are moved quickly, and the player decides which cup the ball is under. In terms of status codes, we will achieve this by creating a random number generator that will produce either the number 1, 2, or 3. These are our branches used in the logic app. State 1 will be used to indicate success. State 2 will be used to cancel the logic app. State 3 will be used to generate an error state. After several runs, the states will populate on our management report, and from there, we can identify where the problem is and how many times the issue has occurred.

Exercise – creating a random generator to simulate logic app states

What we will do here is to find a way to create the different outcome states to test runs. This will give you experience with logic app branching, covered in *Chapter 11, Fine-Tuning Logic App Runs with Run After*. Follow the given steps:

1. In the **MatthewtestRG** resource group, click the **+Add** button to add a new resource.

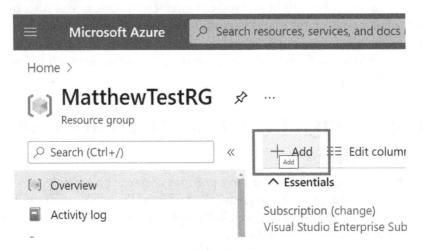

Figure 10.20 – Adding a new resource

2. From the catalog, search for `Logic Apps`. You will notice that as of May 24, 2021, the catalog has changed slightly, and some objects have been re-branded. Standard logic apps are now referred to as **Logic App (Consumption)**. Click the **Create** button to start the wizard.

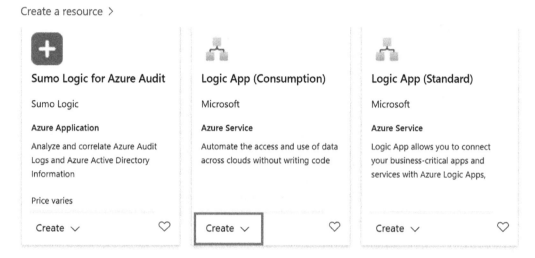

Figure 10.21 – Logic Apps search results from the catalog

3. Complete the **Create a logic app** form as follows:

   A. Subscription: Visual Studio Enterprise Subscription (or whichever subscription you have set up)

   B. Resource group: MatthewTestRG

   C. Logic app name: ShellGenerator

   D. Region: UK West

   E. Enable log analytics: Check

This is what the form should look like:

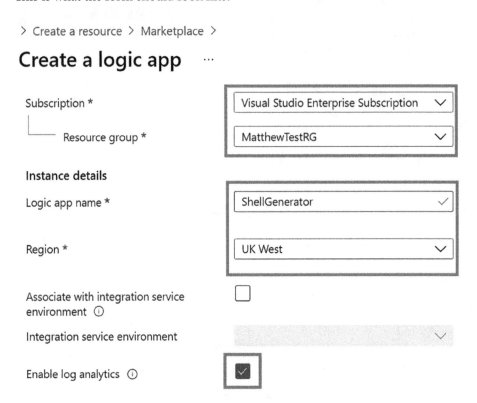

Figure 10.22 – Completing the Create a logic app form

4. Note that the validation will fail if you forget to add the Log Analytics workspace. You need to have created the workspace first to then attach the logic app to that workspace. You can only attach a logic app to one workspace at a time. Select your workspace from the drop-down list.

Figure 10.23 – Selecting the Log Analytics workspace

5. Click the **Review + create** button at the end of the form. This will start the validation process to check for errors or missing information. Once completed, click **Create** to generate the logic app.

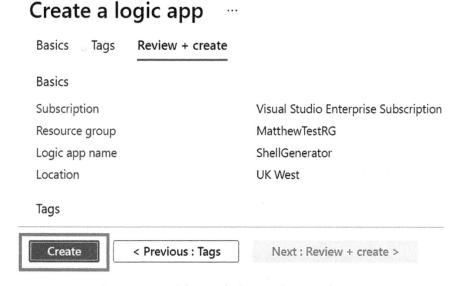

Figure 10.24 – Selecting the Log Analytics workspace

6. Once the logic app has been generated, you will get a notification. Use this to navigate to your new logic app.

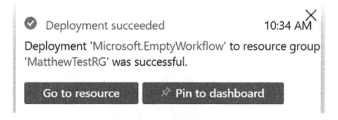

Fig 10.25 – Selecting the Log Analytics workspace

7. Going to the resource will take you to the default *helper* page where you can select a common trigger. We are going to select **Blank Logic App** and build the logic app step by step.

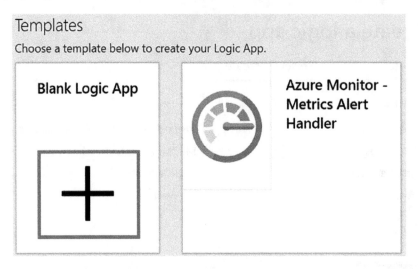

Figure 10.26 – Starting from Blank Logic App

8. We are going to set the logic app to trigger every second once enabled. While editing the logic app, please **Disable** the logic app on the **Overview** page. Let's set the trigger first.

    In the trigger search box, type recurrence. Select the **Schedule** trigger.

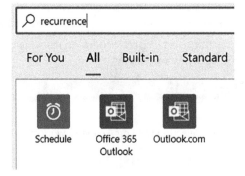

Figure 10.27 – Selecting the Schedule trigger

9. Set the schedule **Interval** field to 1 second.

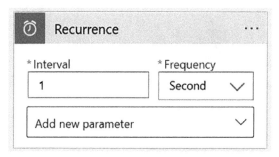

Figure 10.28 – Setting the interval

10. After the trigger, initialize a variable called `stages`. Set the data type to **Integer** and in the **Value** field, from the catalog, select the **Expression** tab. Add the following formula:

```
Rand(1,4)
```

This will generate a random number from the starting number (the first parameter) and up to the maximum number (the second parameter). The result will be values between 1 and 3.

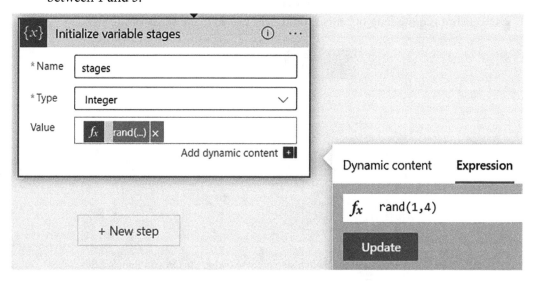

Figure 10.29 – Setting the randomizer

11. Click the + **New step** button and from the catalog, search for `switch`. You will find this in the **Control** section.

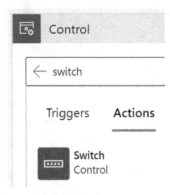

Figure 10.30 – Adding a switch

12. In **Switch**, set the **On** parameter to use the **stages** variable. Click the **Add** button next to **Case branches** to add in two more case branches. Rename these as 1, 2, and 3. In each case branch, add the number to test on in the **Equals** field (so, 1, 2, and 3 respectively for each case).

Here is an exploded view of the **Switch** statement and one of the branches (the screenshot is quite long but this should help you to make sense of the switch):

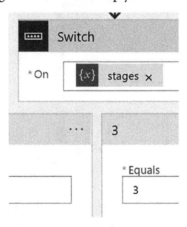

Figure 10.31 – A section of the Switch statement showing the On and Equals fields.
Three case branches have been created

We are going to use option 1 to signify a passed logic app. Option 2 will be for a canceled logic app, and option 3 will illustrate an error state.

13. In case **1**, inside the white area of the tile, click the **Add an action** button. From the catalog, select a **Compose** action. Rename this as `Passed` and add this word in the **Inputs** field.

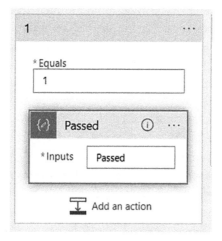

Figure 10.32 – Adding the Passed compose message

14. For case **2**, click **Add an action** and this time select the **Terminate** control. Change the status to **Cancelled** and rename the control as `Cancelled`.

Figure 10.33 – Adding the Cancelled termination action

15. For case **3**, add a **Terminate** action just as for case **2**. This time, set **Status** to **Failed** and rename it as `Failed`. It is not necessary to add an error code or a message, but you can if you wish to. Save your logic app and return to the **Overview** page.

16. On the **Overview** page, enable the logic app for approximately 1 minute, then disable it to avoid unnecessary costs. You should see a random sequence of **Succeeded**, **Cancelled**, and **Failed** logic app runs.

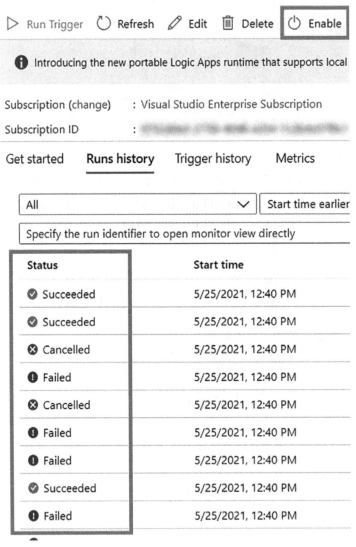

Figure 10.34 – Enabling/disabling the logic app and a series of run states

Go back to the **Resource group** page for **MatthewTestRG** and you will notice the logic app workspace solution object has now been created (**matthewrglaw**). Open this and you will have a high-level view of logic apps that have Log Analytics running. As we have only enabled this for one logic app, the results will be for this one logic app, although usually, you would use this dashboard to look at all logic apps in the resource group.

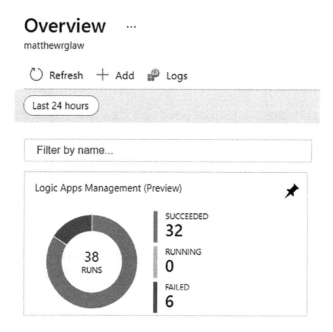

Figure 10.35 – High-level view from the matthewrglaw workspace

This shows that over a period of **24 hours**, **38** runs were monitored, of which **6** failed. It does not count canceled runs on this screen.

Go back to your logic app and enable it, then return to this screen and refresh – you should see at least 1 running.

> **Tip**
> The average runtime for this logic app is 108 milliseconds, so it fires and completes too quickly to notice on the dashboard. If you had more complex logic apps that take several seconds to complete, they would be listed as running on this workspace.

By clicking on the chart, you will get a breakdown of the logic apps used, runs by status, and actions/triggers that are causing an error.

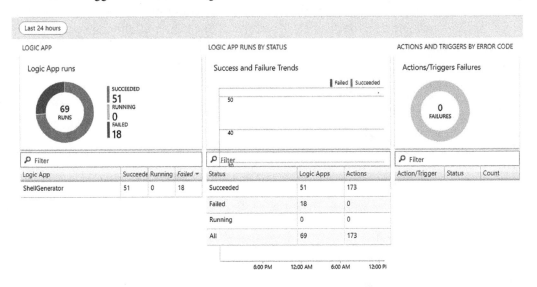

Figure 10.36 – Summative view from the MatthewRGLAW workspace

The dashboard is extremely useful – not only do we get an overview of the health of the resource group, but we can drill into specific details, bulk-run failed runs, and explore failed run IDs. To do this, we can look at the management report that sits behind this dashboard, which is covered in the next section.

Creating a management report and navigating it to find an error

Now that we have the summative view with data populated from our logic app, click on the **Failed** line of the **Success and Failure Trends** table. This will bring up a list of failed runs. If you know which runs need to be rerun and, for example, you had an infrastructure error such as a locked table on your database SQL server that the logic app uses, or an API call to your on-premises network and the web gateway was temporarily down, you are safe to rerun the logic app. This can be done in bulk from this table.

Here is the left section of the failed runs table:

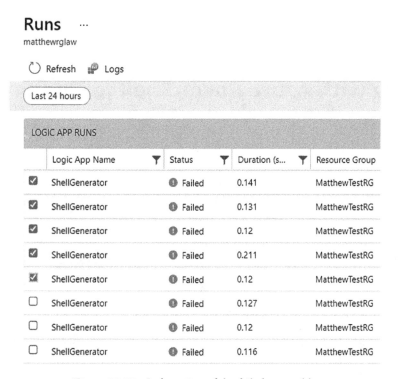

Figure 10.37 – Left section of the failed runs table

Notice that you can select specific logic apps on this table (highlighted in blue in the preceding screenshot).

The right side of the table also has a **Resubmit** button, which allows you to rerun these in parallel.

Tip

Be careful when running logic apps in parallel. If you are making SQL queries, Dataverse queries, or API calls, you might create a bottleneck. If this happens, then other runs will be affected and may time out. I try to keep the number of batched runs to 5-10 but it depends on the logic within the logic app. Our **ShellGenerator** logic app contains no calls or queries, so it is safe to run a higher number within the batch.

While there are several ways in which the workspace can help us to determine what is currently happening within the resource group, where batch processing is required, logic app management is typically done using Azure PowerShell, which we will cover in the next section.

Working with Azure PowerShell for bulk operations

Azure PowerShell is a complex and involved topic – in fact, it is a whole book in itself! What I wanted to do here, however, is to introduce to you one very useful command I use when I want to enable or disable every logic app in my resource group at the same time. I currently manage over 80 logic apps in some resource groups, so to do this manually means that the process is prone to error – I might miss one accidentally.

Exercise – enabling/disabling all logic apps in a resource group

Let's start with the code, then I will explain how it works:

```
1. param([string] $subscriptioname, [string] $resourcegroup,
[string]$state)


2. Connect-AzureRmAccount

3. Get-AzureRmSubscription -SubscriptionName Visual Studio
Enterprise Subscription | Select-AzureRmSubscription

4. Find-AzureRmResource -ResourceType "microsoft.Logic/
workflows" -ResourceGroupNameContains " MatthewTestRG" |
ForEach-Object {Set-AzureRmLogicApp -ResourceGroupName
$_.ResourceGroupName -Name $_.Name -State Enabled -Force}
```

The paper copy of this book will have a black and white graphic here. However, the PowerShell ISE uses common, standard colors as a convention to determine the different elements that comprise a PowerShell script. I will provide examples from the preceding code in the key that follows.

This code is in fact four actions, one after another. I will explain the colors first as this will help you to read the code if you are new to PowerShell:

- **Green** – This is a data type (`[string]`).

- **Dark blue** – This is a parameter (`param`).

- **Blue** – This is a PowerShell function (`Find-AzureRmResource`).

- **Red/Brown** – This is data for a parameter (a parameter's name if it is being set, or a value stored for this parameter (`MatthewTestRG`)).

- **Black** – This is a parameter name that is part of an object (`$_. ResourceGroupName`).

Line 1 sets up three parameters to store values. These are the subscription name, the resource group, and the state we wish to set.

Line 2 connects PowerShell to the Azure account, which has admin rights over the Azure space. For me, when I run this, a connection window appears and I log in, in the normal way. A connection object is created and is stored in memory at this point. This profile is used by PowerShell to execute commands against the Azure tenant.

Line 3 obtains the Azure subscription details as an object. Also, the returned object is marked as the active subscription in focus for PowerShell to work with (`Select-AzureRmSubscription`).

Line 4 looks complex but isn't too bad. First, we find all logic apps but filter by our resource group. This will return a list of logic apps in scope. Now that we know which ones to work with, we `ForEach` through each one in turn. On each logic app, we apply the `Set-AzureRmLogicApp` command where the resource group name and the logic app name are provided from the earlier list. For each, we set the state of the logic app to `Enabled`. The `Force` parameter is used to disable any `are you sure you want to do this?` prompts, which otherwise would stop this script from working.

By doing this, you can very quickly enable or disable logic apps from a specific resource group. This is useful, for example, when saving costs or applying maintenance and you do not want any rogue or unwanted runs.

Summary

In this chapter, we have focused on the Log Analytics workspace. This is a tool used to monitor and manage your resource group and provides a picture of the number of runs, which runs are failing, and why. By taking a baseline of the number of successful runs within a 24-hour period, you have a metric you can use to compare performance as your resource group grows over time. We then created a logic app to simulate different run states and witnessed these in the workspace. We were able to use the runs table to resubmit failed runs. Finally, we looked at how PowerShell can be used for Azure management and specifically looked at a script to enable/disable all logic apps within a resource group.

By doing this, it will make your life as a developer easier. If you also manage the project, you have a ready-made tool to not only benchmark and determine success factors, but as a developer, you will be able to triage faults that have occurred, allowing you to resolve these in a timely manner.

The next few chapters are going to focus on logic app maintenance and management. We will be considering how to fine-tune your logic apps by using the **Run After** action. We will look at how to solve connection issues and bad gateways by rerunning logic apps. We will look at the default number of retries and when it is not a good idea to rerun API calls. We will also look at how triggers and run IDs can be used to identify Logic Apps runs we may need to inspect. Finally, we will also look at the management reporting of Logic Apps, extending areas covered in this chapter.

Section 3: Logic App Maintenance and Management

While it is easy to work with a logic app once the actions are known and the design process is understood, getting it to work how you expect it to can be a challenge in just the same way that writing modules for your C# app will have different sections that need to be tested. Can a sequence of actions be run in parallel? What would happen if a child logic app timed out? How do I ensure that I am getting the best performance from my app? How many times should I rerun an action? What is the effect of rerunning an action when writing to a file on an on-premises file server?

In this section, we discuss fine-tuning a run, identifying problematic runs using a management reporting tool, and the Runs History page. We also look at how it is possible to, once you have made changes, rerun an earlier run so that this time you get it right, without having to have to resend data again from the source system.

This part of the book comprises the following chapters:

- *Chapter 11, Fine Tuning Logic App Runs with Run After*
- *Chapter 12, Solving Connection Issues and Bad Gateways by Rerunning Logic Apps*

11
Fine-Tuning Logic App Runs with Run After

The process of creating and fine-tuning a logic app depends on knowing what data you are expecting to see, the format you want that data to end up using, and adding conditions to check whether operationally, procedurally, or programmatically related data can also be obtained, manipulated, and used as efficiently as possible. Sometimes, you only want a certain section of a logic app to work if the previous action was successful, failed, or was skipped. By creating different logic branches, you can do different things based on whether the previous action was successful or not.

In this chapter, you will learn the following:

- We will look at when it is a good idea to branch your code, such as when there is no cross-branch dependency on other variables or data. We will also learn how to move from a *series* sequence (one branch) to *parallel* branches, and then how to remerge the branches for further processing.

- We'll consider the main Common Data Service (Dataverse) calls that retrieve records. One will retrieve any number of records that meet the criteria, while the other retrieves one specific record only.

- Some developers like to use variables, but when data is needed for a short amount of time, it is often easier to use a series of **Compose** actions instead, altering the data step by step. However, this can be accomplished in one action using **expressions**.

- By structuring the logic app with several different parallel branches, we can customize them so that only certain branches are used based on the outcome of the parent action.

- We can also use the **Configure run after** setting to deliberately turn off sections of a logic app when testing, so that only a small portion of the logic app runs.

The chapter is structured into the following sections:

- Logic app branches

- Using pass/fail branches and run after

- List records versus Get record

- Composing data in stages versus using expressions

Let's start by looking at how we can run our code more effectively, reducing runtime.

Technical requirements

To work on this chapter, you will need the following:

- A web browser

- An Azure subscription

- A standard Azure logic app containing a trigger of your choice to start the logic app (commonly a recurrence or HTTP request trigger)

Logic app branches

The standard way to write a logic app is to start with a trigger, then work sequentially down through the logic app *in series*. This approach can take longer than anticipated because of the amount of time needed for Common Data Service/Dataverse or SQL queries. When you are communicating with on-premises equipment and systems especially, there can be a delay while Azure performs a handshake with the system. This is especially noticeable if this is the first run of the day as subsequent runs cache connections.

As a rule, if your logic can be diverted into separate strands, attempt to write your logic app to operate *in parallel*. Where you are not referencing data from an entity in other actions, these can be split off to operate in a different *path* or *branch*.

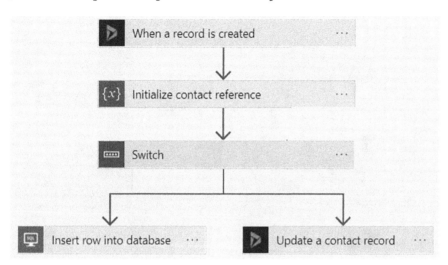

Figure 11.1 – A logic app with two branches

In the preceding example, the trigger is when a record is created. Next, we initialize a variable for later use. We have a switch and dependent on the test on the switch, one of two possible paths will be followed. We then have a split where two branches are actioned at the same time. However, we have limited the scope of the logic app at this point – each branch will only be able to access entities from higher actions. Both can access the trigger and the variable, and the outcomes of the switch, but not each other. I cannot add data from the **Update** action into my SQL row insertion and conversely, I cannot reference the SQL **Insert** query when trying to update the contact record.

It is, however, possible to overcome this by rejoining the branches back together. By pressing the **+ New step** button at the bottom of the logic app, you will create a new action that will be capable of using fields from either branch as well as the original *Series* section at the top of the logic app.

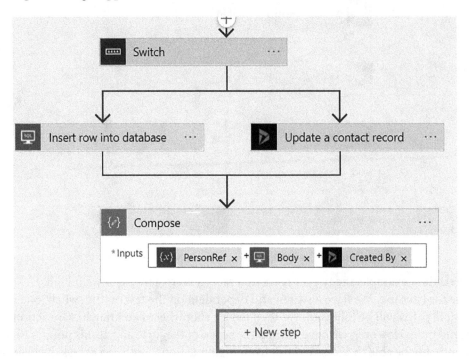

Figure 11.2 – The combined logic app can reference fields from either branch

The main benefit of using branches is that the runtime is reduced dramatically. You can also theme your logic, grouping actions into sections that can run concurrently.

Using pass/fail branches and run after

One other point to note is that branches can be used to determine execution context. By pressing the more button (three dots) on the topmost action in a branch, you can adjust the arrow at the top of the branch to define when data is passed into this branch. The default is to flow data to the action if the subsequent action has a status of **passed**. In other words, if the previous action worked, carry on to the next one below it. However, this context can be changed, as you can see in the following screenshot:

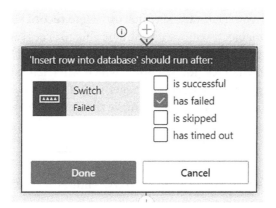

Figure 11.3 – The combined logic app can reference fields from either branch.
Note the arrow has changed to red to indicate a non-default option is in use

Now, only one path will execute. If the **Switch** statement failed, an entry will be added to the database; otherwise, if the **Switch** statement succeeded, the contact is updated in our CRM system, for example, Dynamics 365. This is common practice for auditing actions taking place where you may have dirty data (non-standard data or not conforming to a pattern, or null/empty data where you were expecting a response).

In the next section, we are going to examine how we can obtain records using two actions that are significantly different in how they operate.

List records versus Get record

While they are very similar, the **Get record** and **List records** actions are significantly different in how they are configured. Starting with **Get record**, the primary key (the GUID of the entity) needs to be known in advance. If I, for example, wanted to look up my user account in Dynamics 365, I would reference the environment I am interested in, the **Users** table, and add the **Contact** GUID. This would report back with the full record for that one record.

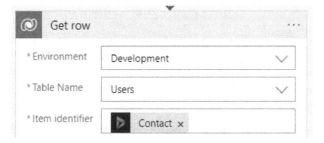

Figure 11.4 – The Get row action uses the primary key of the entity.
This can be hardcoded or accessible based on the contact in scope

You will notice that where you have a trigger such as **Delete record** starting your logic, only the GUID will be available. If you want to still be able to access any data from any fields on the deleted record, you will not be able to. One workaround is to instead use the **Deactivate** button in Dynamics (for example), which will change the state code from active to inactive. By using the Update record trigger with a filter to only fire the logic app when the **statecode** field is changed, you can achieve the same effect but still access the full record.

> **Tip**
>
> With the branding change to Microsoft Dataverse, **entities** are now named **tables** and **records** are now **rows**. I will, however, use these terms interchangeably through this book as some of my actions are Common Data Service and some are Dataverse equivalents.

Therefore, by using the **Get row** action, you can obtain the specific record you are interested in and only that one. This is more efficient than a **List rows** action returning only one record as it is quicker to execute.

Conversely, the **List rows** action, while more powerful in that it acts like a SQL Select query, will return one or more than one records that meet the given criteria. You are expected to create an OData filter query to limit the data to the records in scope, such as the following:

```
First Name eq 'Matthew' AND Last Name eq 'Bennett'
```

Following screenshot shows how **List rows** action filters data:

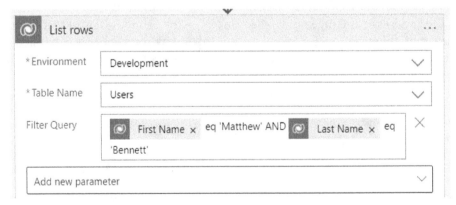

Figure 11.5 – The List rows action uses an OData query to filter the data

The problem with **List rows** is, as with a SQL Select query, we start with every record on the table, then filter down based on the criteria. This has a longer execution time than calling just the specific record we are interested in, as is the case with **Get row**. In the preceding case, what if there were two members of staff called Matthew Bennett? I would get two records in the response. How would I know which was the correct one? Would applying a top count of 1 help here? No – you would get only one record back and it will be the first one found but not necessarily the right one.

List rows actions are, however, very popular as they can, as with SQL Select queries, be expanded to cover related tables where there is a relationship in place.

Composing data in stages versus using expressions

As you progress with logic apps and build up your experience over time, you will undoubtedly get to a situation quickly where you need to look for specific records from different entities where they may be related. One such example might be the contact details for a contact, where the contact details exist not as part of the **Contact** record but in a linked **Contact Types** record. Here, the temptation is to do the following:

1. Make your initial **List records** query to obtain the contact in question.

2. Create a **For each** block cycling through the **Value** field (each record in turn).

3. Inside the **For each** block, create a **List records** query to obtain the contact types for that person.

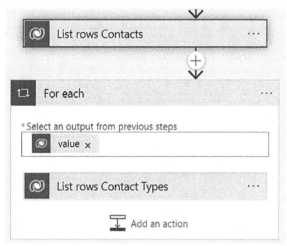

Figure 11.6 – First, we find the contact, and then for each one found, obtain their Contact Type records. This is inefficient

As you can see, this is one call per contact type and one call per contact, which may take several seconds to act.

An alternative would be to create an **Expand Query**. In other words, by including the other related entities in the original OData query, we can perform the action quicker and in only one call to Dataverse.

Available from this link, `https://www.xrmtoolbox.com`, XrmToolBox is a very powerful collection of tools and plugins that can help you to maintain your Dynamics 365 system. Take the example of a CRM system used to track **tenants**; I would first query my contacts and then determine which of these have tenancy contracts related to them. In XML, I would create a filter query looking at the **Contact** table and from these records, expand to the related **Tenancy** table and return where there are matching records:

```
<fetch>
  <entity name="contact" >
    <attribute name="fullname" alias="fullName" />
    <link-entity name="tenancy" to="tenancy_lookup"
from="tenancyid" >
      <attribute name="tenancyno" alias="tenancyNumber" />
    </link-entity>
  </entity>
</fetch>
```

The **FetchXML Builder** tool, found as part of XrmToolBox, would read the preceding XML script, connect to your Dynamics 365 system, and retrieve the records you wanted. Moreover, it can return the OData-equivalent query, which you can then use in the **Expand Query** action.

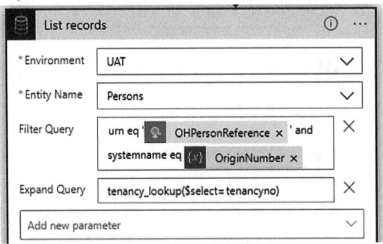

Figure 11.7 – List records with an Expand Query

In the preceding example, the person is filtered to the specific person we are interested in, but the record output will also contain the tenancy data for any related tenancies.

Summary

I was very tempted to write this chapter much earlier in the book but felt that you need to understand the tools before mastering how you can improve logic app performance. In this chapter, you have been able to consider running code in parallel and the benefit of doing this. You have also considered that branching your logic app will also scope the data to entities on the same branch and above the action, as well as to any sections that are not in a branch. You have also learned to use branches that will only be used based on the status of the previous action – if the earlier action failed, follow, and use the **fail** branch. The default setting for all branches is that the earlier action passed. This is referred to as the **run after** state.

We considered a Common Data Service (Dataverse) action called **List rows**, which filters the entity by performing an OData query. Alternatively, we have the **Get row** action, which although similar relies on you knowing the primary GUID for the record you want to return.

Knowing which action is the better of the two will shave several seconds off the runtime of your logic app, plus reduce processing. As a rule, try to only recover records that are needed and simplify your logic, returning only the fields you need. As you progress, you might also like to consider **Expand** queries, which are used to extend your **List records** filter to return fields from related entities, rather than separate **List records** actions for each entity.

The next chapter discusses how to solve connection issues and bad gateways through logic app reruns.

12

Solving Connection Issues and Bad Gateways by Rerunning Logic Apps

When you're trying to communicate with other cloud or on-premises domains, you must authenticate and pass data through a firewall. Logic apps have a timeout window of up to 2 minutes and presume that if no response is received before this time, the data is lost, and the connection can't be contacted. This chapter will look at common connection issues, how to understand them, and how to resolve them. As development is an iterative process, you may need to run your logic apps several times until you are happy with the result. You'll also learn how to rerun **logic app** runs without having to resend the original data from your external system time and again.

In this chapter, you will learn about the following:

- A SQL connection will time out if the logic app does not receive a response within 2 minutes. This could indicate transient problems on the network, firewall, web proxy issues, or authentication errors.

- An on-premises data gateway is an additional step that's added to the SQL profile when you are trying to connect to an on-premises SQL server. If the web gateway to your domain is not present, you will only be able to connect to cloud-based SQL databases.

- As with SQL on-premises connections, on-premises file servers also need to be configured to use an on-premises data gateway. The connection often uses the internal IP address and file path. Typically, there are concerns regarding the number of times we send the message to the file server and the impact this will have.

- HTTP calls are often one way. These calls are to a child logic app, or another module capable of receiving a **GET** message. Once called, the parent logic app can continue without issue. Request API calls, however, require a response. If a response is not received within 2 minutes, then a timeout error message is generated. These are often used when you need to send data back from the child logic app.

- Creating and refining a logic app is an incremental process. As with C# program design, you work on a section of logic and test it to ensure that you obtain the results you are looking for. Once the JSON message has been received, or the logic app has been triggered to operate the original message that was entered, the top of the logic app can be re-presented as many times as needed. There is no need to resend another copy of the message from the originating system. This speeds up the fine-tuning process.

- Each logic app has a **Runs History** table, which you can use to identify the run you are interested in, determine if it was successful or failed, and resubmit it. If you have made alterations to the logic app, the original message will still be used, allowing you to test your new changes.

The chapter covers the following main topics:

- Creating and using SQL databases
- Connecting to a SQL database using an Azure connection profile
- SQL connection timeouts/bad gateway messages
- SQL connection web gateways
- File server connection gateways

Technical requirements

To work on this chapter, you will need the following:

- A web browser.
- An Azure subscription.
- A standard Azure logic app containing a trigger of your choice to start the logic app (commonly, this is a recurrence or an HTTP request trigger).

Creating and using SQL databases

One of the most used connections is a query to obtain or set data from a **SQL database**. Azure has a large variety of database connections in its catalog, but one of the most used is the SQL database. However, before we get on to the subject of timeouts and error messages, we need to understand how SQL databases are created and accessed. First, I will explain this process and get us to a point where we can use a database under normal operations. At that point, I will focus on errors and how to manage them.

Two types of databases are available, and this is determined by where the database is stored. If the database is stored within the cloud, it can be accessed by a connection object in the resource group that has direct authentication, typically by using your Azure service account (or user account, if you're not operating on an Enterprise-level project). As the database is a cloud resource, the account is common to both Azure and the database as a resource, so no additional security to access the database is required.

Exercise 1 – creating an Azure database

In this example, we are going to create a database, set it up with some data, and then access this data via a logic app. Let's get started:

1. In the **Resource groups** section, press the **Create** button to open the creation form:

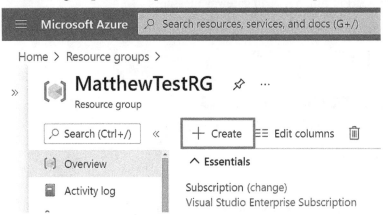

Figure 12.1 – The Create button is used to add a new object to the Resource group

2. In the catalog's search field, search for SQL Database.

3. You will be presented with the **SQL Database Overview** page. Press the **Create** button to start creating this resource:

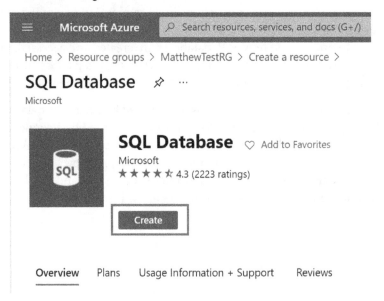

Figure 12.2 – The Create button is used to start the process of creating the new resource

4. On the **Create SQL Database** page, in the **Basics** tab, use the following values:

A. **Subscription**: **Visual Studio Enterprise Subscription**

B. **Resource Group**: *<my resource group>*

C. **Database name**: MyTestDatabase

D. **Server**: sqltestmjb

> Tip
>
> This resource is not an independent object – it runs on a virtual machine;
> a "headless server" that manages and applies the database.
>
> In Azure, server names must contain lowercase letters, numbers, and a hyphen.
> They cannot start or end with hyphens and their names must be shorter than
> 63 characters.

E. **Server admin login**: *<your username>*

F. **Password**: *<your password>*

G. **Confirm Password**: *<your password>*

H. **Location**: *<your closest region>*

5. Press **OK** to continue.

6. On the **Database details** page, confirm that the database's name and the server are correct. If you are on a budget and do not need to worry about performance, you can share a SQL elastic pool to reduce costs between your resources. If you only have one database or want this database to have dedicated resources, do not select this option.

7. In the **Configure** section, set a pricing plan that suits your budget. I have selected a **Basic** plan with a data size of 100 MB as this is going to be a small database that's used for testing purposes. Once you have selected the plan you are looking for, click the **Apply** button.

8. When considering backup storage redundancy, you have options for **Locally redundant**, **Zone-redundant**, or **Geo-redundant** storage. These relate to where you would like the database to be backed up. There are legal implications for storing your data abroad and laws differ from country to country, so please be selective and choose an option that is right for you. As this is test data and I am not overly concerned about the data in my database, given that it is not corporate-sensitive, I have left this as the default option (**Geo-redundant**). When you're ready, press the **Review + create** button.

9.   You will then be informed of **Security and Additional settings**. Note that the settings shown are the default settings. You can use *Azure Storage Explorer* or *SQL Server Management Studio* to manage these later. When you are ready, press the **Create** button:

> **Tip**
> The default collation (character set used) is **SQL_Latin1_General_CP1_CI_AS**. If you are managing a website that requires a backend database, such as for a shopping cart, you may need to alter the collation to an alternative that does or does not support Unicode/non-Unicode symbols if you wish the website to be used internationally.

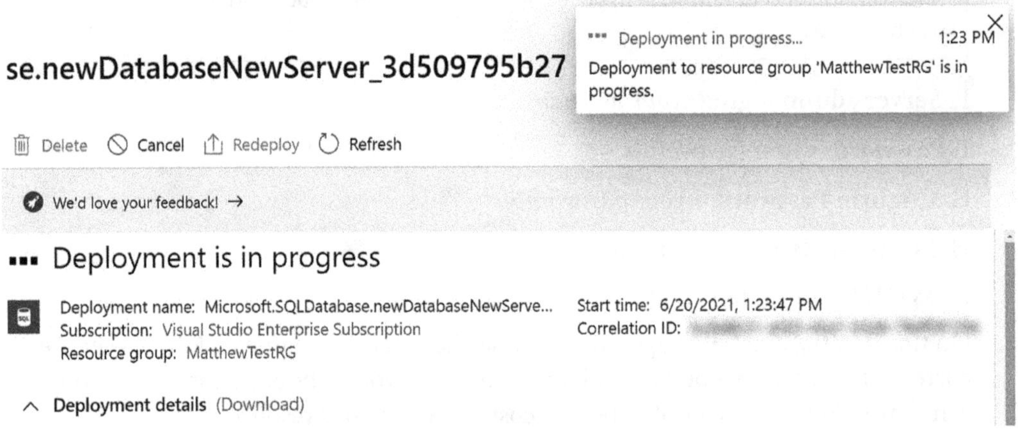

Figure 12.3 – Your database is being deployed

This process will take a few minutes. At this point, the virtual machine is being deployed and the database is being created on it. Eventually, you will see a **Deployment succeeded** message, at which point you can directly access the new database. Press **Go to resource** to visit the new database's **Overview** page.

Here is our new database:

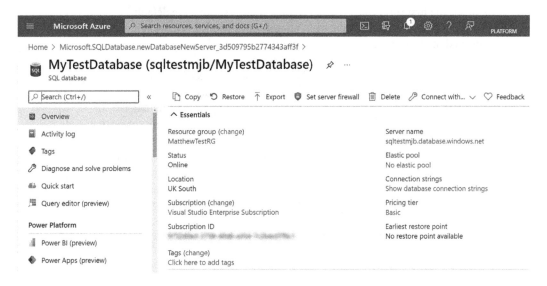

Figure 12.4 – The new database is ready for use

By completing this exercise, you have provisioned your first Azure SQL database.

Creating our first table – possible with Query Editor?

In this example, we are going to use **Query Editor**. This is a new feature that's recently been added to Azure so that you can make changes without the need for desktop software such as **SQL Server Management Studio** (**SSMS**).

On the **Overview** page, on the left blade, select **Query Editor (preview)**. You will see the following page:

> **Tip**
>
> As this is the first time you are accessing this new resource, the default security stance is to block traffic from all unknown users, even though you requested the resource be made. This may seem counter-intuitive, but you must remember that the only action we've undertaken so far was to provision this resource, and that was done by a Microsoft service account, not your user account. You will need to introduce your Azure workspace and your user account to the server. To do this, you will notice that upon loading Query Editor for the first time, you get a security message with a hyperlink suggesting that you either log in using your Azure account or allow a firewall rule to be created to accept the IP address you are using. This will be added to the Azure firewall and allow access to the database server. Once you click on this hyperlink, you will be authenticated, and Query Editor will open as normal.

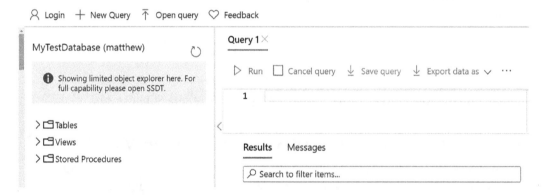

Figure 12.5 – The new, albeit limited, Query Editor

At this point and despite my hopes that Query Editor will eventually allow us to discount desktop apps, I am still going to need to use either **SSMS** or **Visual Studio** to be able to manage the database. Let's connect using Visual Studio.

Exercise 2 – creating the table using Visual Studio

Sticking with our tried and tested Visual Studio, we will create the table design structure (schema) and populate it with some test data. Let's get started:

1. On your PC, open *Visual Studio*.

2. We do not need to create a project as we will not be storing any local files. Click the **Continue without code** link:

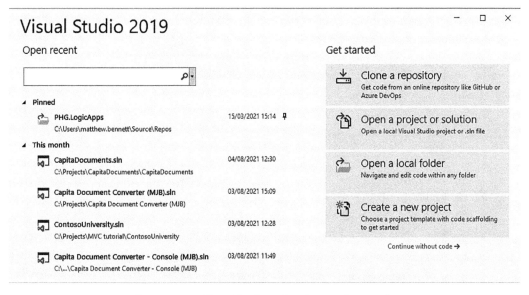

Figure 12.6 – Visual Studio – Continue without code

3. From the top menu, select **View** > **Cloud Explorer**:

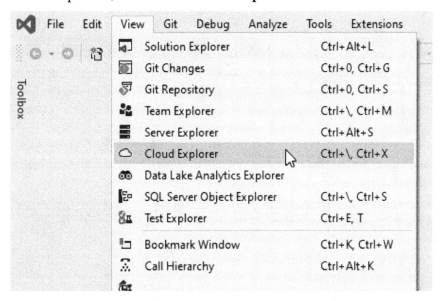

Figure 12.7 – This is where Cloud Explorer can be found

4. In the **Cloud Explorer** pane, select the subscription you have used. You will find the new database we created earlier:

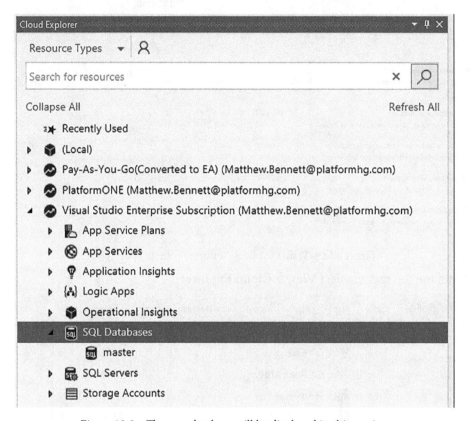

Figure 12.8 – The new database will be displayed in this section

5. Right-click on the new database and select it to open this database using **SQL Server Object Explorer**.

6. You will be prompted with a connection form. Supply the necessary password and press the **Connect** button to attempt to connect:

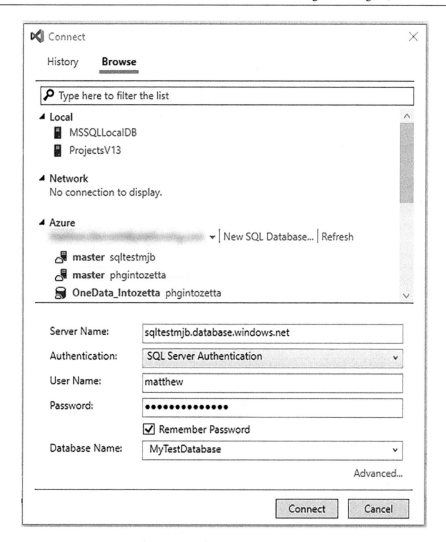

Figure 12.9 – The Connect form in SQL Server Object Explorer

> **Tip**
>
> As this may be the first time in a while that your PC has connected to your Azure account, you will be prompted with a question – do you want to add your IP address to the Azure firewall, thereby allowing you access to the database? Yes, of course you do want this, but please ensure that you do say "Yes" at this point; otherwise, you will block yourself from accessing the database at all and this can be VERY hard to undo. In fact, it would be quicker to delete this one and start again.

7. In SQL Server Object Explorer, from your database, go to **expand Tables**. Right-click and select **Add new table…**.

8. You will now be presented with a schema editor. We are going to make four fields, like so:

Name	Data Type	Allow nulls	Default	Primary Key
Id	int	No		Yes
Firstname	nchar(20)	Yes		
Lastname	nchar(20)	No		
CustomerType	nchar(20)	No		

Table 12.1

These can be represented by the following SQL command:

```
CREATE TABLE [dbo].[Table]
(
    [Id]  INT NOT NULL PRIMARY KEY,
    [Firstname] NCHAR(20) NULL,
    [Lastname] NCHAR(20) NOT NULL,
    [Customertype] NCHAR(20) NOT NULL
)
```

9. Press the **Update** button at the top left to make this alteration to the database.

10. You will be presented with a preview window. Use the **Update Database** button to make this change:

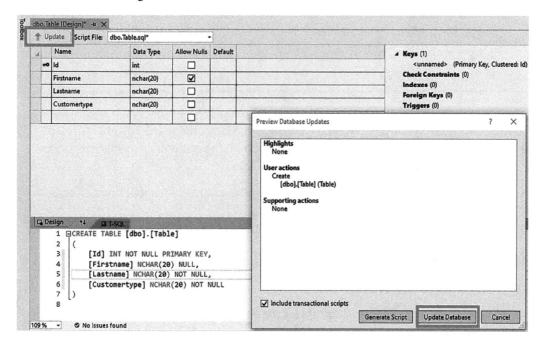

Figure 12.10 – Committing the table creation in SSOE

After a few seconds, the update will be complete.

11. In the SSOE pane, you will see that our new table has been created in the **Tables** folder. Its default name is dbo.Table. Right-click this to rename it dbo. MyTable.

Please remember that you can only rename the table if you have closed any windows that are using this table first.

> **Tip**
>
> SQL table names are in two parts. The first section is the schema. This is a naming system that's used to separate tables into separate namespaces. By doing this, you can use the same table name in different namespaces, like so:
>
> a. `Project1.MyTable`
>
> b. `Project2.MyTable`

When you rename the table, only the table's name is displayed – the schema itself will have to be changed, which you can do by altering the Master database. For reference, the Master database is used by the SQL engine to catalog all the other tables, as well as the system-generated tables that form part of the database.

Now that we've finished creating and using SQL databases, let's talk about connecting to a SQL database using an Azure connection profile.

Connecting to a SQL database using an Azure connection profile

Now, let's use Azure to connect to this table. I am going to create a new logic app that will create rows in our database. Create a blank logic app with an HTTP request for the trigger. Then, add a new action. In the catalog, look for *SQL* and select **SQL Server category**. From the list of actions, select **Insert row**.

If you already have a connection profile you can use that to point to the correct server, select it from the list. We don't need to press the **Add new** button in our case to make a new connection profile.

On the first profile page, set **Connection name** to something memorable, such as `MatthewTestConnection`. In this case, we will be using **SQL Server authentication** to authenticate the connection by using the details from the **Connection** profile we created earlier.

Here is my completed **Connection** profile:

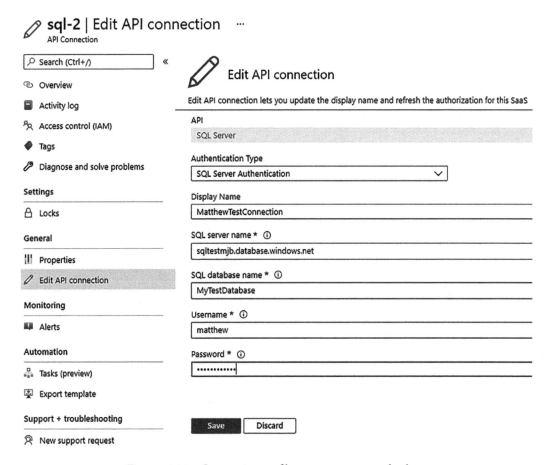

Figure 12.11 – Connection profile to access our new database

You will be prompted to sign in. Please sign in with the credentials you used when creating the database earlier.

You will probably get a message stating that the IP address that was used was not authorized. Afterward, you will be asked to update your firewall settings. Let's do just that.

In a new tab, navigate to the database's **Overview** page in Azure. Press **set server firewall** to access the **Firewall settings** profile page:

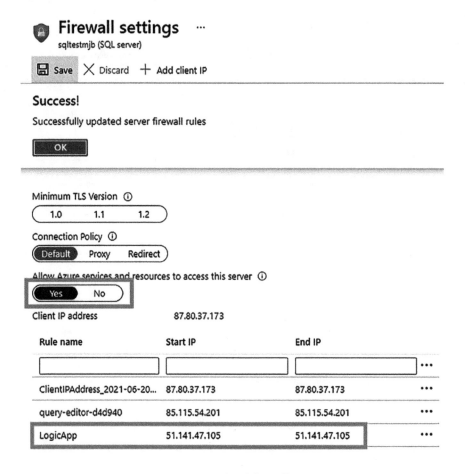

Figure 12.12 – Updated firewall settings

You will notice that I have taken the extra step to allow Azure services to access this server. This allows the database to be accessible from the logic app.

Returning to the logic app, we can now complete the connection portion of the **Insert Row** action. This will appear like so:

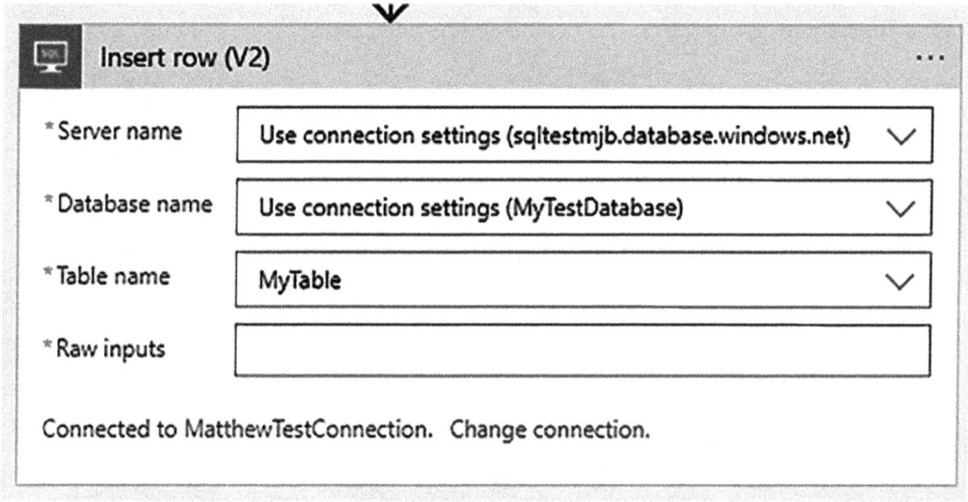

Figure 12.13 – Completed connection profile for the Insert row (V2) action.
This only appears the first time the action is used

Once saved, the action changes and a **Raw inputs** field will be available. This field expects your new row as a JSON message.

Were you expecting to see a list of fields? The reason you are not seeing a list of fields is that the logic app has not read the table schema yet. This is done when the logic app is executed. Running this field with a blank or incorrect JSON message will cause an error and no data will be saved (the action will not complete), but in doing so, the fields will be cached and the next time we visit this action, the fields will be populated on the form correctly.

Here is the correct JSON message if you want to get it right the first time:

```
{
            "Customertype": "Customer",
            "Firstname": "Matthew",
            "Id": 1,
            "Lastname": "Bennett"
        }
```

Notice that the message order does not need to match the table field order.

Here is the **Insert row** action after one execution has been made:

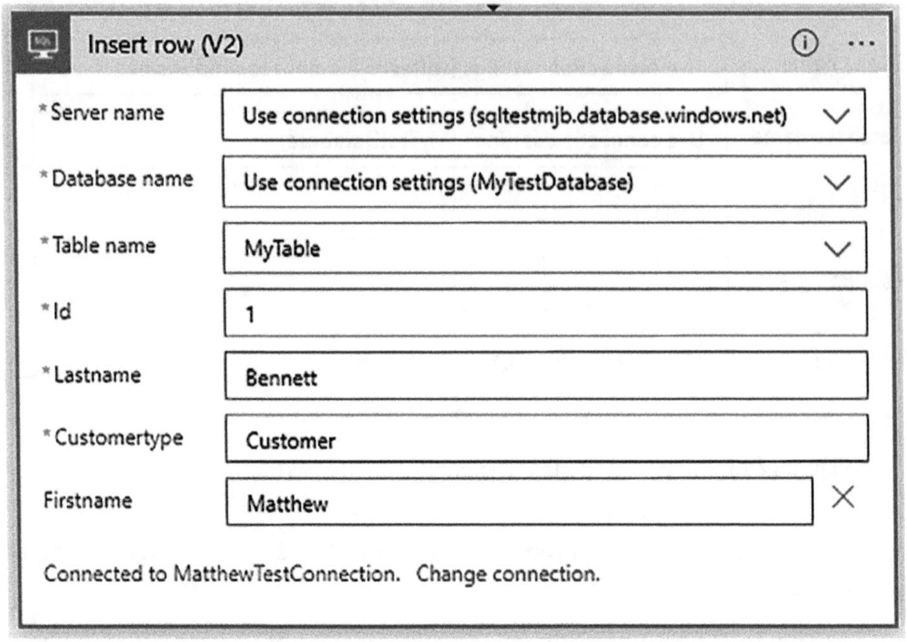

Figure 12.14 – Completed Insert row (V2) step with fields displayed this time

Now that we know how to use SQL databases, let's discuss SQL timeouts and bad gateway messages.

Understanding SQL connection timeouts/bad gateway messages

When working with SQL queries or **Insert/Update** statements, you will find that the action is reasonably reliable. However, when you are connecting to an on-premises server that is part of the infrastructure, there may be several points of failure, not including the database server itself, which may be busy. Requests will be queued, and other queries may have exclusive access, meaning that your request will have to wait. Once the wait window has elapsed (typically, the default is 2 minutes), the request may retry if you have set the policy to do this, or the action will mark it as a failure.

Connection wait timeout errors

If you are running a complex SQL query or script that takes a long time to process (if the logic app has not heard back within 2 minutes), the logic app may produce an error, along with a timeout message:

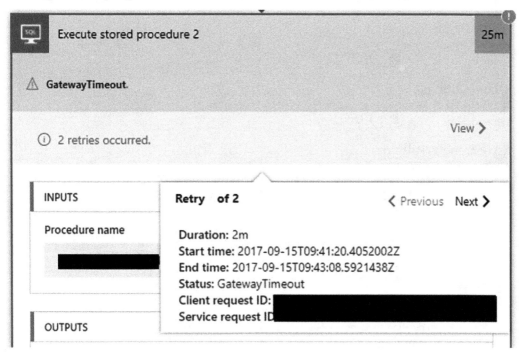

Figure 12.15 – Standard gateway timeout message

If you ever experience this and are convinced all is well, the best course of action would be to split the logic app into two. End the logic app with an instruction so that the processing takes place remotely. Then, you can send the output in the form of a JSON message to the second logic app, which can carry on with the process.

Alternatively, you can go back to **Logic App Designer**, press the **More** button (the three dots at the top right of the action), and select the **Settings** pane:

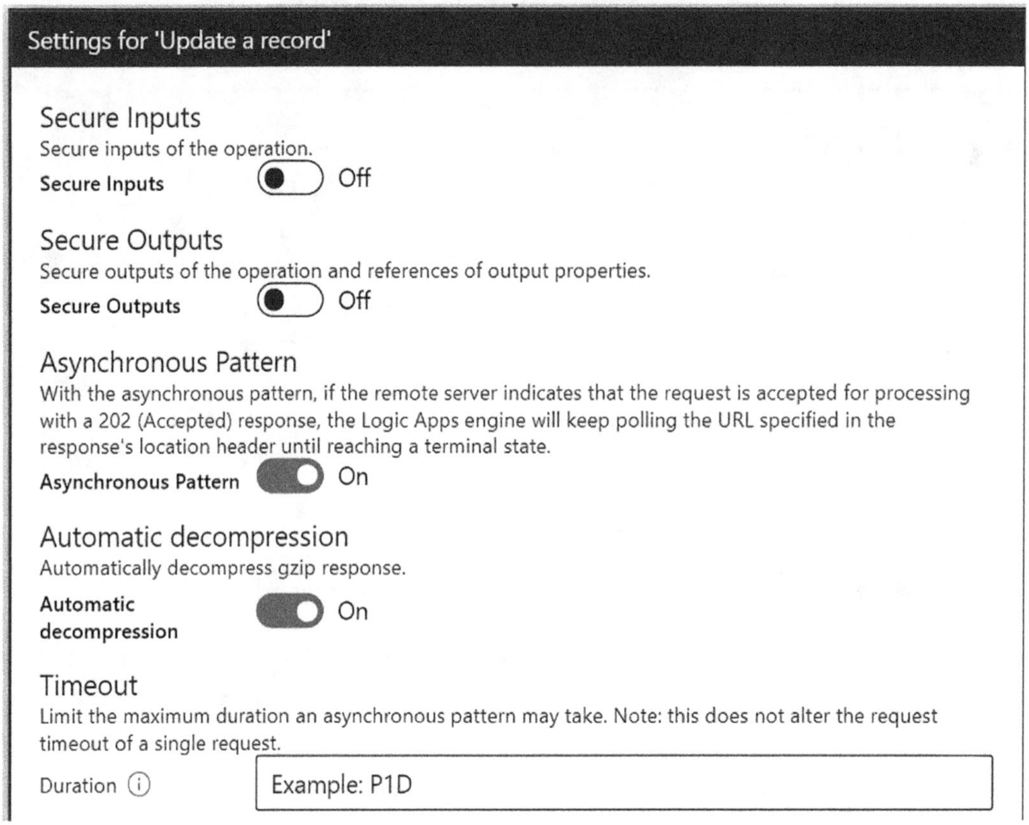

Figure 12.16 – Settings for the 'Update a record' action with Timeout displayed

On the **Settings** page, you will see a **Timeout** option. This overwrites the 2-minute default wait time with one that's more useful for your needs. You must specify the timeout in ISO 8601 format, so use the following template:

P(n)Y(n)M(n)DT(n)H(n)M(n)S

So, 40 minutes would be written as PT40M.

However, this would only really work if you were actioning this action multiple times, such as in a **Foreach** loop. If run as a single action, the timeout will not be used.

> Tip
>
> Microsoft advises that if you are planning to run a long-running script, you should put it into a separate child logic app and use request/response actions to return a 202 message immediately to the calling parent logic app. By doing this, the parent can continue with other work while the child logic app, specifically designed for the long-running task, can proceed separately.

Bad gateways

A bad gateway message is slightly different in that it's more concerning but also quite common, especially when you are trying to connect to an on-premises server. Here, breaks in the infrastructure, server reboots, locked tables, and application locks on the web proxy server will hamper your connection to your end resource, namely the database you are trying to access. These problems are often transitory, but they still require you to rerun the logic app at a later point in time, once you have managed to test that you have connectivity to the resource.

SQL connection web gateways

To connect with the on-premises network, a perimeter network proxy server or third-party supplier account is required. This provides a heavily secured access point in the form of your corporate network's public-facing IP address. The job of the proxy is for it to be configured with a set of rules to determine if the incoming traffic is from a trusted source and using a trusted connection port. From here, it can route the traffic internally to our local, on-premises database server. Here, we are establishing an end-to-end, encrypted, authenticated tunnel that allows Azure resources to access and be accessible from the on-premises network.

Creating a web gateway to an on-premises network is beyond the scope of this book, but I will point out how to add one to your connection profile, should you intend to access on-premises resources:

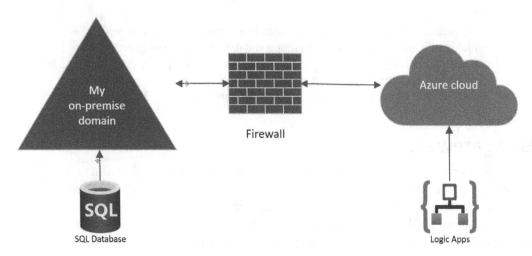

Figure 12.17 – Infrastructure diagram explaining the association between cloud and on-premises resources

If we create a new SQL connection profile but this time select **Windows Authentication** as the connection type, then we have the option to connect via a connection gateway. Presuming that you created a gateway beforehand, you will be able to access your resource using the connection gateway profile you have set up previously.

> **Tip**
> You can only use an on-premises gateway with an organization ID. You cannot use a personal trial account for this.

Typically, you would use the **Windows Authentication** profile because this will use the on-premises Active Directory account to authenticate you to the gateway and the database:

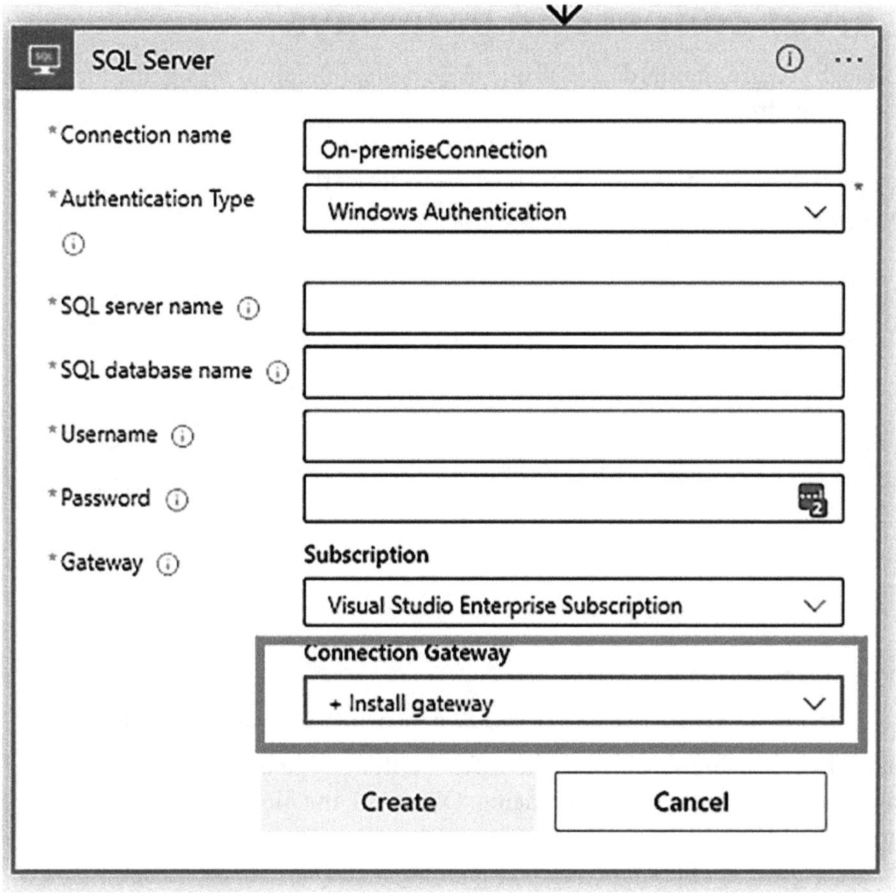

Figure 12.18 – A new SQL connection profile containing the option for a connection gateway

Now, let's discuss SQL connection web gateways.

File server connection gateways

Quite archaic by Azure standards and prone to be quite difficult to set up, the file server connector acts in almost the same way as the SQL connection. There are two groups of file actions: **Azure file storage** and **traditional file storage** (for on-premises use). Both share the same green icon, and it is a common mistake to select the wrong one. If your files are stored in an Azure storage account, then you will want to set up a connection to that account and use Azure file storage:

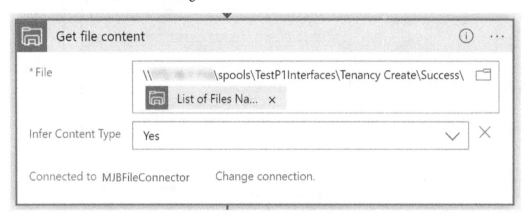

Figure 12.19 – The Get file content action will retrieve the payload of a file

Note that in the preceding screenshot, the **Infer Content Type** option can be used to understand the type of file we are referencing. Obtaining the file's content is useful when you are planning to add the file as an attachment to an email or save a copy of the file as Azure will determine the file's type (such as an image) and save it accordingly.

Summary

While the main aim of this chapter was to show you how to work with connection errors and timeouts from different types of resources, I simply could not pass up the opportunity to explain how to create a SQL database, a table, a connector, and how to add data to these first. I hope you have found this to be a rewarding and helpful chapter. Since I have been working with these actions daily and often, I find that issues on my daily logic app management report tend to be those concerning transient connection problems. Most of the time, where the data is not time sensitive, I am safe to retry by rerunning the logic app.

In the next chapter, we are going to look at default retry policies and how neglecting to set them correctly may not only impact the performance of your logic, but duplicate records unnecessarily in your database and increase your expenditure costs!

`Packt.com`

Subscribe to our online digital library for full access to over 7,000 books and videos, as well as industry leading tools to help you plan your personal development and advance your career. For more information, please visit our website.

Why subscribe?

- Spend less time learning and more time coding with practical eBooks and Videos from over 4,000 industry professionals

- Improve your learning with Skill Plans built especially for you

- Get a free eBook or video every month

- Fully searchable for easy access to vital information

- Copy and paste, print, and bookmark content

Did you know that Packt offers eBook versions of every book published, with PDF and ePub files available? You can upgrade to the eBook version at `packt.com` and as a print book customer, you are entitled to a discount on the eBook copy. Get in touch with us at `customercare@packtpub.com` for more details.

At `www.packt.com`, you can also read a collection of free technical articles, sign up for a range of free newsletters, and receive exclusive discounts and offers on Packt books and eBooks.

Other Books You May Enjoy

If you enjoyed this book, you may be interested in these other books by Packt:

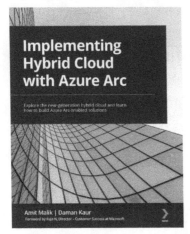

Implementing Hybrid Cloud with Azure Arc

Amit Malik, Daman Kaur

ISBN: 9781801076005

- Set up a fully functioning Azure Arc-managed environment
- Explore products and services from Azure that will help you to leverage Azure Arc
- Understand the new vision of working with on-premises infrastructure
- Deploy Azure's PaaS data services on-premises or on other cloud platforms
- Discover and learn about the technologies required to design a hybrid and multi-cloud strategy
- Implement best practices to govern your IT infrastructure in a scalable model

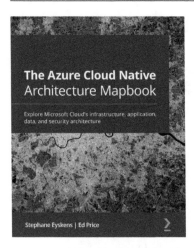

The Azure Cloud Native Architecture Mapbook

Stéphane Eyskens, Ed Price

ISBN: 9781800562325

- Gain overarching architectural knowledge of the Microsoft Azure cloud platform
- Explore the possibilities of building a full Azure solution by considering different architectural perspectives
- Implement best practices for architecting and deploying Azure infrastructure
- Review different patterns for building a distributed application with ecosystem frameworks and solutions
- Get to grips with cloud-native concepts using containerized workloads
- Work with Azure Kubernetes Service (AKS) and use it with service mesh technologies to design a microservices hosting platform

Packt is searching for authors like you

If you're interested in becoming an author for Packt, please visit authors.packtpub.com and apply today. We have worked with thousands of developers and tech professionals, just like you, to help them share their insight with the global tech community. You can make a general application, apply for a specific hot topic that we are recruiting an author for, or submit your own idea.

Share Your Thoughts

Now you've finished *Enterprise Integration with Azure Logic Apps*, we'd love to hear your thoughts! Scan the QR code below to go straight to the Amazon review page for this book and share your feedback or leave a review on the site that you purchased it from.

https://packt.link/r/1-801-07472-0

Your review is important to us and the tech community and will help us make sure we're delivering excellent quality content.

Index